THE TYRANNY
OF THE MERITOCRACY

THE
TYRANNY
OF THE
MERITOCRACY

DEMOCRATIZING
HIGHER EDUCATION
IN AMERICA

LANI
GUINIER

Beacon Press
Boston

KH

BEACON PRESS
Boston, Massachusetts
www.beacon.org

Beacon Press books
are published under the auspices of
the Unitarian Universalist Association of Congregations.

18 17 16 15   8 7 6 5 4 3 2 1

This book is printed on acid-free paper that meets the uncoated paper
ANSI/NISO specifications for permanence as revised in 1992.

Text design and composition by Kim Arney

Library of Congress Cataloging-in-Publication Data

Guinier, Lani.
    The tyranny of the meritocracy : democratizing higher education in America /
Lani Guinier.
        pages   cm
    Includes bibliographical references and index.
    ISBN 978-0-8070-0627-6 (hardback)
    ISBN 978-0-8070-0628-3 (ebook) 1. Education, Higher—Aims and
objectives—United States. 2. Education, Higher—Social aspects—United States.
3. Democracy and education—United States. 4. Multicultural education—
United States. 5. Discrimination in higher education—United States.
6. Minorities—Education (Higher)—United States. I. Title.
    LA227.4.G85 2015
    378.1'9820973—dc23

                                                        2014027507

11/18/15

CONTENTS

INTRODUCTION

SUSPENDED ON STEAM tunneling up from the government-issue heating grates, the last of the fall foliage dances just beyond the windowpane. In the crisp autumn air, the leaves ricochet off the grimy glass before coming to rest on the banks of the buildings' curved cement ledge, just outside the science classroom. These dancing leaves are barely visible to the sixteen- and seventeen-year-old teenagers unpacking their book bags atop rows of smooth, black Formica countertop, crowded with petri dishes, glass beakers, and gas blowtorches. It's a Monday morning in November, the time of year when high school seniors around the country carefully calculate their college admissions odds. A solemn stillness reigns as nine boys and one girl wait for the Advanced Placement physics teacher to begin the double-period lesson that is the toughest course in this public school. Of the seven high school seniors and three juniors, only one—a policeman's son—does not have parents who graduated from college. Nevertheless all ten students are preoccupied with the same thing: getting into college.

"Who remembers what the force on a turning object is called?" The teacher surveys the room as he toys with a piece of chalk.

A hand from the front row shoots up. "Torque!" cries the son of a computer engineer. Wisps of his tousled, orange hair outline his pale face, suddenly ruddy with his excitement.

The teacher nods. The boy beams. He quickly swivels in his chair to note the reactions of his classmates. Annoyed by their tired, first-class-of-the-day expressions, he glances back toward the teacher for approval, but the teacher has already returned to the blackboard. Undeterred, the boy blurts out, "Oh, I'm so smart."

The class seems amused but mostly inattentive. A few students suppress yawns. The others busy themselves trying to find the right page in the textbook. A deep cough from the back of the room breaks the silence. The proprietor of the cough, the policeman's son, wears an ironic smile. He has rocked his chair back to rest against the countertop right below the gas blowtorch. Jutting out his chest he bellows, "You shouldn't say that about yourself!"

"I can," the first boy says with a sneer. A smug grin spreads over his face. "I can," he repeats, "when I got a 1600. Bitch." (Today a perfect score would be a 2400.)

A loud thump echoes through the classroom as the front legs of the second boy's chair hit the floor. His eyes narrow. The smile on his face dissolves in a brew of contempt and hurt.

The orange-haired boy's sly excuse has worked. He was proud to know the answer to the teacher's question; but his real agenda was to broadcast his perfect SAT scores. Except for the scraping of the chalk on the blackboard, the room is quiet.

But unable to contain his enthusiasm, the braggart with the orange locks interrupts the class several more times, proclaiming his flawless SAT scores again and again. Awe morphs into disgust among his classmates, yet no one else speaks out. The policeman's boy squirms. He sits hunched with his elbows cocked on his desk, his stubby fingers cupping his chin.

Finally, after the fourth unanswered SAT-score announcement, the policeman's boy sits straight up, his face still glowering from the earlier insult. "That's enough," he snarls. "Shut up already about your scores."

Another student, a tall, long-limbed boy, enters the fray. His parents both graduated from an Ivy League college, and his dad is a science professor. This leggy fellow chewing on a pencil has said nothing all class, but he now pitches forward in his chair as he calmly assumes the role of defense attorney for the braggart. "If I got a 1600," the college professor's boy says, "I'd be talking about it too."

The policeman's son grimaces. His lip curls as he reluctantly acknowledges the shifting classroom alliance. It is now two against one. He plants his hands on the desktop. "Maybe so," he mumbles and briefly contemplates the thought that the SAT creates a special exception for crude boasting.

"But it doesn't mean you have to be a jerk," he finally shoots back.

For the immodest boy who has hit the SAT jackpot, there is no difference between accomplishment and arrogance. In the terminology of the SATs, a 1600 (or a 2400, depending on what year the test was taken) is an achievement worthy of mentioning—several times. Indeed it is such an accomplishment that it cries out for mention not just by the boy with the perfect scores but by his peer advocate as well.

Both the boastful boy and his tall, lanky supporter know the game. The rules, so the thinking goes, are objective, neutral, and, above all, fair. And that boy won. Using the SAT test as a yardstick, college admissions officers select who they think are the best-prepared students, meaning those likely to get the highest first-year grades. Presumably the SAT not only measures college preparedness; it also provides an incentive system for high school students to work hard and take a rigorous curriculum. The tenets of high-stakes admissions testing—the testocracy—have become so widely shared that they form the building blocks of a secular religion among college-bound elites: if you test well, you deserve to enter a top college. In some ways you have earned the right not just to succeed but to preen. And, such students might think, you owe nothing to anyone, not to the community whose tax dollars supported your AP physics lab with a teacher/student ratio of one to ten, and not to your classmates, whose own egos and futures are also on the line.

The testocracy, a twenty-first-century cult of standardized, quantifiable merit, values perfect scores but ignores character. Indeed, the boy with the winning scores, derisive grin, and bad manners could be a poster child for the closely fought college admissions competition.

The testocracy teaches the cocky boy to internalize success and to take personal credit for the trappings of privilege, including the educational resources and networks of his college-educated parents. He has learned that individual achievement trumps collective commitment. Those who reach the finish line faster will reap their rewards here on earth. And one of those rewards is the right to brag.

The boy still squirming with resentment in the back row knows the difference between being proud and being a jerk. He has the instincts of character. One should not boast, preen, or complain. Yet, he knows that, to the academic world, his character counts less than his SAT scores. He knows that the SAT opens doors to the best schools and by extension to long-term success. This boy is from a working-class family. The son of the policeman and the school secretary, he is hoping to be the first in his family to attend college. But in order to give himself and his children-to-be a better life than his parents could provide for him, he needs financial aid. He plays hockey, but because he barely got 1300 on his SATs, his athletic skill was not enough to win a much-needed scholarship. Thus far he is losing in the college admissions contest. His test scores and his self-esteem both take a beating. Reduced to protesting from the back row, he struggles to compete while staying grounded. His parents cannot afford SAT prep classes. He will simply retake the test, hoping that his scores improve.

THIS IS THE challenge I propose in this book: to reconsider the status quo. We can and must adjust our understanding of testocratic merit to better reflect what we want to value in a democratic society. Testocratic merit makes the assumption that test scores are the best evidence of applicants' worth, without paying much attention to the environments in which one finds those individuals. It thereby ignores several built-in biases that privilege those who are already quite advantaged. However, if our society truly values education as a means of preparing citizens to participate in the decisions that affect their lives as individuals and the society they create as a collective, as well as to enable individuals to improve their lots and their society, then we need to reexamine exactly how we define "merit."

Harvard economist Amartya Sen defines "merit" as an incentive system that rewards the actions a society values.[1] Defining merit through students' grades and test scores is evidence that our society values individual competition above all else. As the policeman's son reminds us, our obsession with testing is often depressing but it need not be permanent. In fact, the historical journey that led to this current culture, which I trace in chapter 2, demonstrates how our national understanding of "merit" can change and has changed over time. We are at a turning point in history. It is now time for another culture shift: from honoring testocratic merit to honoring democratic merit.

We can alter how we think about merit, from something a child is born with to something that she (and/or we) can help cultivate. We can shift from prioritizing individualized testing to group collaboration among all stakeholders, including students, parents, teachers, and administrators. Unfortunately, it's not going to be easy, as the entire undergirding of our educational system rests upon notions of individual achievement and the promotion of competition. Yet we must shift from promoting testocratic merit, which has produced dubious results, to developing democratic merit, because the latter is the foundation upon which our national values truly ought to rest.

I am not trying to destroy the concept of merit here. I am trying to redefine what it means to be meritorious beyond a student's performance on standardized tests or in isolated academic situations. If we are going to have a "meritocracy"—which really just means "rule by merit"—then we need a better conception of what now constitutes merit in our society versus what it should be.

THE TERM MERITOCRACY was coined by British sociologist Michael Young as a spoof. In his 1958 satire, *The Rise of Meritocracy, 1870–2033*, Young gave an imaginary account of a smug elite: instead of ancestry, ability had determined their social position. Rule by this select few would appear both benign and bountiful because of a talent-based formula for assigning status. The best would rise to the top using this simple equation: intelligence (or aptitude) + effort = merit. In Young's hypothetical meritocracy, test scores (or other suitable substitutes for innate talent or aptitude) would matter the most; because those who had risen in the status hierarchy would have attained their status through talent and effort, they would also be immune to criticism. Those at the top of this status hierarchy would be able to justify their continued rule because they had earned it.

To Young, such a testocracy would not be a shining vision but rather a nightmare. And more than forty years after the publication of his book, Young is "sadly disappointed" at how the word he coined has "gone into general circulation, especially in the United States."[2] He intended to warn society about what might happen if, in assigning social status, we continued to place gaining formal educational qualifications over all other considerations. In Young's fictional world, anyone unable to jump through educational hoops, including many—like the policeman's son—from the working class, would be barred from a new, exclusive social class as discriminatory as older ones based on inheritance.

And that is exactly what has happened. Through their admissions criteria, our colleges and universities have adopted Young's nightmarish meritocracy. Just as Young anticipated, merit as defined by test-based admissions has harnessed "schools and universities to the task of sieving people" according to a "narrow band of values."[3] Those values, as it turns out, are the production and reproduction of privilege but without obligation or shame. The rise of the testocratic meritocracy has enabled those already at the top of the heap to continue to preside without a sense of moral or political accountability. The privileged have come to believe that their "advancement comes from their own merits," and thus they are entitled to their power.

But this is not the only possible definition of merit. The term *merit* originally meant "earned by service."[4] Giving good service, such as working for the benefit of community rather than simply for personal advantage, is what made someone worthy of entitlements, such as admission to top-ranked colleges and plum internships and job opportunities. Democratic merit revives this notion by providing educational access to those who serve the goals and contribute to the conditions of a thriving democracy. It does what our current meritocracy fails to do: it creates an incentive system that emphasizes not just the possession of individual talent and related personal success but also the ability to collaborate and the commitment to building a better society for more people. Our nation has always prided itself on overthrowing tyranny. We now have a new one in our midst: the tyranny of our current understanding of meritocracy.

PART I

THE PROBLEM

CHAPTER ONE

Adonises with a Pimple

MANY BOOKS HAVE been written on the failings of the American education system. The recommendations to fix these problems are quite varied and include the development of a national curriculum, giving teachers fair wages, ensuring that teachers are involved in the decisions of central administration, and encouraging extensive family involvement in students' lives. And these are just the suggestions found in one author's book.[1]

The idea I'd like to advocate in this book, however, is simple but powerful: we need to change our understanding of merit. Currently, merit is measured by an individual's test scores and grades. The higher the test scores and the better the grades, the more entitlements are granted to an individual by teachers, parents, administrators, other students, and even the general public. But this need not be the case. Instead, I've found that what is urgent for our world—and thus what we should consider most closely in education—is a student's capacity to collaborate and to think creatively. Here I intend to explore the current meritocracy in America and how it developed along with the rise of the SAT and other supposedly objective metrics used to evaluate a student's candidacy for college.

In the next section of this book, I will propose a new framework, one focused on advancing democratic rather than testocratic merit.

This section draws upon a number of case studies—most in the field of education, but not always—to demonstrate how teamwork and the fortification of strong collaborative relationships can achieve the ends that will serve our society best in the long run.

IN 2012, UNIVERSITIES, businesses, advocacy organizations, and communities of color held their breath as they waited for the Supreme Court to decide *Fisher v. University of Texas at Austin*. The case had been brought by white University of Texas applicant Abigail Fisher, who argued that the university's race-conscious admissions program was unconstitutional because it had denied her admission on account of her race. As the public awaited a decision, many feared that the case would threaten the future of race-conscious admissions policies, despite the fact that ten years had passed since the Supreme Court had decisively upheld the constitutionality of affirmative action in *Grutter v. Bollinger*.

So when the Supreme Court finally released its opinion in the *Fisher* case, on June 24, 2013, proponents of affirmative action breathed a sigh of relief. The majority opinion (which will be covered in greater depth in the next chapter), authored by Justice Anthony Kennedy, was anticlimactic, even reassuring. Issues of diversity were still on the table; the opinion had not dismantled affirmative action altogether, as most had feared.[2] Justice Clarence Thomas agreed with the majority, albeit on different grounds. He wrote separately to argue that affirmative action and any consideration of race in admission should always be unconstitutional.[3] In fact, Thomas argued, all attempts by a university to achieve diversity among its students were exactly the kind of racial discrimination that had maintained segregation, because it meant the university was considering race in the first place.[4]

According to Thomas, then, any naming of race was tantamount to racial bigotry. He described race-conscious admissions as a type of "discrimination [that] has a pervasive shifting effect" because the "University admits minorities who otherwise would have attended less selective colleges where they would have been more evenly matched."[5] Thomas went on to write, "As a result of the mismatching, many blacks and Hispanics who likely would have excelled at less elite schools are placed in a position where underperformance is all but inevitable because they are less academically prepared."[6]

Justice Thomas's argument—what we might call the "mismatch effect"—is a stark reminder that our universities have drifted away from their public mission to create active citizens in a democratic society. They have shifted their attention, instead, to that single moment in a student's college (or law school) experience: the moment of admission. If, as Justice Thomas argues, students must only be admitted to places that "evenly match" them, what responsibilities are left to higher education? In Justice Thomas's formulation, universities perform little more than sorting functions, cherry-picking students who have come up the escalator of excellence and arrive at their doorsteps presumably pre-packaged and pre-equipped with everything they need for success.

This drift from a mission-driven to an admission-driven higher education system should give all of us pause. I, for one, have had formative, nurturing educational experiences that made me a better, more inquisitive, more accomplished student than I was at the moment of admission. It should also give Justice Thomas pause, because Thomas himself was the beneficiary of mentorship and thoughtful guidance during his college years at Holy Cross. Justice Thomas has acknowledged the important role his mentors played in creating an environment of challenge and support that allowed him to reach his educational goals. As such he is a poster child, reminding us that the duty of our universities is to give students an educational experience in which merit is cultivated, not merely scored.

In arguing that students should arrive at college "evenly matched" to the school's standards for excellence, Clarence Thomas seems to have forgotten that when he arrived as a sophomore transfer along with nineteen other freshmen at Holy Cross in the summer of 1968, Father John Brooks, a dean, student advocate, and mentor at the college, had personally written up files on each of them, highlighting what set them apart from other young men. Father Brooks had identified each of the men's strengths: some had challenging family backgrounds that they had already shown signs of overcoming; others had exhibited a willingness to push beyond expectations and give back to their communities in big and small ways.[7] Father Brooks believed that the black students may not have been fully prepared for Holy Cross, but more importantly—more urgently—he felt that Holy Cross was woefully unprepared for them.[8]

One evening in the autumn of 1968, Clarence Thomas came knocking on Father Brooks's door. He had come by to discuss some classes, but the conversation turned quickly to many larger questions, including Thomas's feelings of alienation as he adjusted to college and his anxieties that his grades would not secure him a spot at an Ivy League law school.[9] Brooks listened with an open heart and then assured Thomas that he could find within himself the ability to succeed, not only at Holy Cross but in the future as well. Father Brooks promised Thomas that he would always hold him to high standards, but that if Thomas were to find something too difficult, Brooks's door was open for them to talk and find a way.[10]

During Thomas's years at Holy Cross, he found himself knocking on Father Brooks's door quite frequently to talk with his mentor about coursework, campus life, and current affairs.[11] After graduation, Thomas did attain his goal of attending an Ivy League law school, and at Yale Law he dreamt about using his legal career to "right the wrongs of segregation."[12] During one of his law school summers, thanks to a fellowship that I helped him obtain, Thomas interned at a civil rights law firm in his home state of Georgia, and began a legal career that ultimately brought him to a seat on the Supreme Court.[13]

There is, in other words, both a direct and an indirect conflict between Clarence Thomas's own lived experience and his criticisms of college admissions and affirmative action. This conflict is not just limited to Justice Thomas; Thomas's current view of the way college and graduate school admissions in America should work is a widespread cultural tradition. Admissions to post-secondary education in Canada provide a stark contrast to the American system. In Malcolm Gladwell's *New Yorker* article "Getting In," he tells his own story of how, as a Canadian teenager, he applied to universities in his country. He recalls filling out an application one evening after dinner where he spent "probably . . . ten minutes" ranking his preferred universities. He vaguely remembers filling out a supplemental list of interests and activities, and sent that in. His high school sent in his grades; there was no need for an SAT score or to ask anyone to write letters of recommendation. "Why would I? It wasn't as if I were applying to a private club," he recounts.

Admitted to his first-ranked school, Gladwell, in the article, said he considered it an odd question as to whether he considered himself a better or more successful person for having been accepted there, as opposed to his second or third choice.

> In Ontario, there wasn't a strict hierarchy of colleges. . . . But since all colleges were part of the same public system and tuition everywhere was the same (about a thousand dollars a year, in those days), and a B average in high school pretty much guaranteed you a spot in college, there wasn't a sense that anything great was at stake in the choice of which college we attended. The issue was *whether* we attended college, and—most important—how seriously we took the experience once we got there. I thought everyone felt this way. You can imagine my confusion, then, when I first met someone who had gone to Harvard.[14]

To illustrate the difference in approach represented by the United States and Canada, Gladwell uses the analogy of a modeling agency versus the Marine Corps. The Marine Corps, Gladwell writes, "doesn't have an enormous admissions office grading applicants along four separate dimensions of toughness and intelligence. It's confident that the experience of undergoing Marine Corps basic training will turn you into a formidable soldier."[15] Modeling agencies, on the other hand, sign on recruits because they are already beautiful.[16] Applying these ideas to university selection processes, Gladwell argues that the "extraordinary emphasis the Ivy League places on admissions policies . . . makes it seem more like a modeling agency than like the Marine Corps."[17]

Professors Robert Paul Wolff and Tobias Barrington Wolff pose a similar argument in a law review article published a few months before Gladwell's *New Yorker* piece. In it, they paint a picture of the tiny imaginary island republic of "Invertia."[18] The father-son author duo then take the reader on hypothetical visits to two of Invertia's preeminent national institutions: a world-class hospital and a top-flight university. In the hospital's emergency room, the visitor sees two patients: one suffering from an apparent heart attack and one complaining of a small pimple on his nose. Unexpectedly, the emergency room staff leaves the heart attack victim to die, turning its attention to the second man, a tall, tanned figure whom the Wolffs call "a veritable Adonis" (referring to the legendary Greek god of beauty). The Invertian minister of health, who goes to the hospital with the Wolffs, has this to say in defense of the doctors' choice of treatment:

> Every so often, we see a patient who is obviously bursting with good health and natural physical gifts—fit, vigorous, strikingly attractive. When such a patient comes along, needing only the very slightest medical adjustment to emerge in perfect condition, a patient with whom our chance of success is virtually one hundred percent, we are prepared to waive the normal procedures and speed the admission process. . . . Invertian society needs an elite core of superbly healthy men and women whose every last imperfection or blemish has been meticulously removed by the most modern techniques of medical science.

Admissions procedures at the university, however, are quite the opposite. There, the Wolffs describe the university admissions office's summary rejection of a straight-A scholar-athlete who, in her free time, performs as a concert pianist and volunteers with inner-city and dis-abled youth. An underachieving, semi-literate young man is chosen in her place as a member of the incoming class. The university representa-tive explains its decisions:

> [The] young woman is already so well developed intellectually that she does not need what an elite university can offer. . . . To spend the scarce educational resources of our top university on her would be wasteful and inefficient. . . . Educationally speaking, if I may put it this way, [the young man] was in extremis when he walked in. . . . At this very moment, our team of professors is working with him, start-ing the painful, difficult process of developing his intellect, challeng-ing his mind, helping him work through the shame and self-doubt of semi-literacy. . . . Imagine the thrill we all feel when one of those young people, whose mind had all but ceased to exhibit curiosity and creativity, begins to read, to write, to think, to argue, to question a world that has, until then, been closed to him.

The authors use the fantasy nation of Invertia to show two stark al-ternatives: a world in which resources are used to improve even further those in near-perfect health versus one in which even the lowliest of citizens are given the tools to cultivate their intelligence in order both to have the opportunity to excel and to contribute to their society. I find it extremely disturbing that our universities resemble more closely the hospitals that take in classes full of Adonises to treat them for a pimple on the nose than they do mission-driven universities that are engaged in educating and nurturing all of their students.

You might think I am exaggerating. I wish I was. It is a shock to discover that the doctors of Invertia, preoccupied with Adonises, are everywhere. When I went to the Yale campus to see my son graduate I picked up a copy of the student newspaper, which had published a profile of the graduating class. I scanned it with interest (looking for mention of my son, of course!) when I came across a chart called "By the Numbers." The undergraduate class of 2009 was described this way:

BY THE NUMBERS **UNDERGRADUATE CLASS OF 2009**	
1,321	Students in the original freshman class
157	Students in the original freshman class with alumni parents
750	Median SAT Verbal score
740	Median SAT Mathematics score
9.7	Percent of applicants admitted
113	Number of international students

I tried to figure out what was bothering me so much. Eventually it struck me: every single one of these statistics that the paper was celebrating reflected student achievements or demographic facts, all of which were established before the students even got to New Haven! It was as if the entire Yale College experience had been nothing but a confirmation of high school scores, as if it were a finishing school run by a modeling agency. Where was a list of the students' accomplishments as a result of their college experience? Where was evidence of the college's own self-described mission of educating future leaders and citizens of a democracy?

Yale and other elite institutions such as Harvard and Princeton are private institutions. Yet despite their generous endowments and steep tuition rates, they are still subsidized by state taxpayers. Many are situated on land that the public donated. Their faculty receives public subsidies through research grants, and their students receive a disproportionate amount of federally financed scholarship funds. This subsidy occurs despite the fact that the majority of their enrolled students are wealthy. Colleges such as the "Big Three"—Yale, Harvard, and Princeton (but not limited to these three by any means—offer enormous opportunity to a few, while largely avoiding their obligation to the many by taking an increasingly scarce public reservoir of riches and making it available primarily to those who can pay. The result? Predictable. Anyone who wants to play the game has to shift their attention from the mission declared by our country's elite institutions of educating future leaders and citizens of a democracy to the goal of gaining admission to their storied halls.

In his recently published book, *Crazy U: One Dad's Crash Course in Getting His Kid into College*, journalist Andrew Ferguson astutely describes the frenzy that accompanies the college admissions process today. As he comically recounts his experience helping his son apply— and get in—to college, Ferguson laments:

> What had once been a fairly brief and straightforward process, in which the children of the middle and upper classes found a suitable college, filled out an application, got in, and then went happily away, returning home only now and then to celebrate holidays and borrow money, has evolved into a multiyear rite of passage, often beginning before puberty.[19]

This rite of passage, Ferguson says, carries with it a probability of ultimate success that is "much worse than a crapshoot."[20] Frankly, I'm not familiar with the game of craps, but these odds don't sound very good. We could also compare getting into college to entering the lottery (something all Americans can relate to)—except it is not random, like state-sponsored lotteries. Instead, the odds of winning in this lottery are stacked in favor of the Adonises of our world, the children of the wealthy.

In a 2014 *Boston Globe* article, Beth Teitell describes one seventeen-year-old high school senior whose extracurricular activities, designed to make him attractive to the college of his choice, were padded to the point of absurdity. The student had "studied electrical engineering at Skidmore College, argued in mock trials at Columbia University, developed apps at MIT, and screened patients for tuberculosis in Thailand."[21] Teitell rightly identifies that "with college tuition an enormous financial stress for many families, adding pricey summer programs to the tab is something that's out of reach for most people, who see resume-building activities as yet another example of wealthy families trying to buy their children advantages."[22] And nowhere is the gap between what the haves and the have-nots can do for their children to help them get into college more visible than in the test-preparation courses that presumably ensure that most notable attainment of the American Adonis: a high SAT score. The SAT, as the preeminent standardized test for college admission in the United States, best reflects our national obsession with the moment of college admission, rather than with the post-graduation missions of those who attend our colleges and universities. This despite the fact that SAT scores are accurate reflectors of wealth and little else.

Are your no. 2 pencils sharpened?

CHAPTER TWO

Aptitude or Achievement?

A special lottery is to be held to select the student who will live in the only deluxe room in a dormitory. There are 100 seniors, 150 juniors, and 200 sophomores who applied. Each senior's name is placed in the lottery 3 times; each junior's name, 2 times; and each sophomore's name, 1 time. What is the probability that a senior's name will be chosen?[1]

DOES THIS KIND of question look familiar? For most of you, it probably does: it represents just one of the nearly two hundred questions that presently make up the SAT.[2] (The answer, by the way, is 3/8, or 37.5 percent, for those among us who prefer percentages to fractions.) For nearly a century, universities across the country have used SAT scores and other quantifiable metrics to make decisions about admitting one candidate versus another—decisions that can have far-reaching impact on both the admitted and declined candidates' educational, social, professional, and financial futures. On the basis of what? we might ask. Originally the acronym SAT stood for Scholastic Aptitude Test, on the strength of the argument that a high schooler's success on the test correlated with his or her success in the increasingly rigorous environment of college. As evidence of this correlation dwindled, the name was changed first to the Scholastic Assessment Test (keeping the handy, well-known acronym) and later to the SAT Reasoning Test. Call it what you will, the SAT still promises something it can't deliver: a way to measure merit. Yet the increasing reliance on standardized test scores as a status placement in society has created something alien to the very values of our democratic society yet seemingly with a life of its own: a testocracy.

Allow me to be clear: I'm not talking about all tests. I'm a professor; I believe in methods of evaluation. But I know, too, that certain methods are fairer and more valuable than others. I believe in achievement tests: diagnostic tests that are used to give feedback, either to the teacher or to the student, about what individuals have actually mastered or what they're learning. What I don't believe in are aptitude tests, testing that—by whatever new clever code name it goes by—is used to predict future performance. Unfortunately, that is not how the SAT functions. Even the test makers do not claim it's a measure of smartness; all they claim is that success on the test correlates with first-year college grades, or if it's the LSAT (Law School Admission Test), that it correlates with first-year law school grades.

As I'll explain later, such a correlation is slight at best. In any case, it's certainly not a barometer of merit. Merit is much too big a concept to simply refer to how you're going to do in your first year of college or law school. Because if all we cared about is how well you do in your first year of college, we would have college programs last only one year, right? Why would you have to be there and pay tuition for three more years? We do and we must care about more than freshman-year grades—we care about whether students learn something in college, whether they grow into themselves on the way to becoming better citizens and making their distinctive contributions to society. What we really care about are all the things that the testocracy can't measure.

How then did we get to a place where American higher education appears more concerned with applicants' test scores and alumni financial contributions than with the education of current students and the contributions of alumni to our society as a whole? A review of America's curious history of—and relationship with—an obsessive culture of testing may help answer these questions.

—⚅—

"MANLY, CHRISTIAN CHARACTER." That was the ideal that Endicott Peabody, a member of the New England Brahmin class, hoped to cultivate in the boys who attended his private boarding school, Groton.[3] Peabody founded Groton in 1884 with the purpose of building character and embedding the value of "noblesse oblige" into the social fabric of late-nineteenth-century America.[4] Groton students, like young men from seven other boarding schools in the northeastern United States, were to embody character, manliness, and athleticism.[5] The "Big Three" colleges—Harvard, Yale, and Princeton—validated these ideals by admitting nearly all boarding-school applicants and conferring honorary degrees upon Peabody.

Admission into the "Big Three" was fairly easy if the applicant possessed a "manly, Christian character." He had to pass subject-based entrance exams devised by the colleges, but the tests weren't particularly hard, and he could take them over and over again to pass. Even if a student didn't pass the required exams, he could be admitted with "conditions." Once enrolled at Harvard, Yale, or Princeton, he would focus primarily on his social life, clubs, sports, social organizations, and campus activities, while often ignoring his academic work.

Admissions began to change, however, when Charles William Eliot became president of Harvard in 1869. Annoyed with "the stupid sons of the rich," Eliot sought to draw into the university's fold capable students from all segments of society. To ensure that smart students could attend Harvard regardless of their means, Eliot, in 1898, abolished the archaic Greek admission exams that were popular up until that time. He also replaced Harvard's admissions exams with exams created by the College Entrance Examination Board because it tripled the number of locations where applicants could be tested. The result of Eliot's changes was the admission of more public school students, including Catholics and Jews.

A. Lawrence Lowell, Eliot's successor, attempted to reverse the trend of admitting those without WASP status and values. The "Jewish problem" in particular alarmed Lowell. The number of Jews at Harvard had increased steadily, from 10 percent in 1909, to 15 percent in 1915, to 21.5 percent in 1922. In addition to their growth in numbers, Jews generally outperformed non-Jewish students academically. Lowell worried that Harvard might suffer the same fate as Columbia, which experienced "WASP flight" as more Jewish students started to enroll. In response, Lowell limited freshman enrollment to one thousand and altered the admissions criteria to include an emphasis on "character," legacy, and athleticism rather than solely on academic achievement. Additionally, the application process now required interviews and photos, as well as letters of recommendation. Initially a method to limit Jewish enrollment, the notion of a "well-rounded" applicant was born in the first half of the 1920s.

But altering admissions criteria to benefit socially desirable students was not enough for Harvard. With an increasingly complex university admissions process, a new and uniform system was needed to separate the wheat from the chaff. The SAT became the solution that the ruling elite had been desperately seeking for all this time to perpetuate itself: a testocracy, disguised as a meritocracy.

THE ORIGINS OF the SAT can be traced to the turn of the twentieth century, when the College Board, the nonprofit organization that owns the rights to the modern-day SAT, administered the nation's first college entrance examinations, in 1901.[6] Unlike today's SAT, these exams were entirely composed of essays that required students to engage with subjects as far-ranging from each other as Latin, world history, and physics.[7] The birth of these exams came at about the same time as another social scientific phenomenon: intelligence testing.

In 1905, French psychologist Alfred Binet developed the world's first IQ test, which aimed to produce a set of predictable results from which one could "derive a rating of . . . 'mental age'" and "identify slow learners [who] could be given special help in school."[8] Binet's theories were eventually adapted by the United States military during World War I, when Harvard professor and IQ-test advocate Robert Yerkes convinced Army brass to allow him to evaluate nearly two million soldiers to identify top talent who could be promoted to the rank of officer.[9] The results were striking: according to Yerkes, "The native-born scored higher than the foreign-born, less recent immigrants scored higher than more recent immigrants, and whites scored higher than Negroes."[10] In 1923, Carl C. Brigham, a Princeton psychology professor and leading figure in the growing anti-immigration movement of the time, authored a treatise titled *A Study of American Intelligence*, in which he relied heavily upon Yerkes's findings to conclude that "American intelligence is declining, and will proceed with an accelerating rate as the racial admixture becomes more and more extensive."[11]

This belief, which Brigham helped to perpetuate, was lampooned by F. Scott Fitzgerald, a Princeton graduate, in his novel *The Great Gatsby*, published two years later, in 1925.

> "Civilization's going to pieces," broke out Tom violently. "I've gotten to be a terrible pessimist about things. Have you read 'The Rise of the Colored Empires' by this man Goddard?"
>
> "Why, no," I answered, rather surprised by his tone.
>
> "Well, it's a fine book, and everybody ought to read it. The idea is if we don't look out the white race will be—will be utterly submerged. It's all scientific stuff; it's been proved. . . .
>
> "This fellow has worked out the whole thing. It's up to us, who are the dominant race, to watch out or these other races will have control of things. . . .
>
> "This idea is that we're Nordics. I am, and you are, and you are, and—" After an infinitesimal hesitation he included Daisy with a slight nod, and she winked at me again. "—And we've produced all the things that go to make civilization—oh, science and art, and all that. Do you see?"
>
> There was something pathetic in his concentration, as if his complacency, more acute than of old, was not enough to him any more.[12]

The College Board selected Professor Brigham to spearhead the design of a new, nationwide college entrance exam,[13] and on June 23, 1926,

Brigham oversaw the very first administration of what was then called the Scholastic Aptitude Test.[14]

News of the SAT's success eventually made its way up to Cambridge, Massachusetts, where James Bryant Conant presided as president of Harvard University (from 1933 to 1953). Unlike many of his peers at the time, Conant openly embraced the Jeffersonian ideal of a "natural aristocracy of talents and virtue"[15]—a forerunner of the twentieth-century idea of the meritocracy. In 1934, Conant assigned two of his assistant freshman deans, Henry Chauncey and Wilbur J. Bender, the task of identifying high-performing middle-class and ethnic-immigrant students for the possible receipt of need-blind scholarships to the university.[16] The two men offered up Brigham's SAT as the optimal screen through which eligible candidates could be filtered. Conant accepted their recommendation, mandating that applicants take the test in order to be considered for scholarships.[17]

A battle that had begun with idealistic rhetoric succumbed to a Trojan horse: the SAT and a budding testocracy confirmed the existing order as inevitable, because the tests demonstrated that the elite possessed unassailable merit. Harvard's adoption of the SAT subsequently set a new gold standard in the world of education.[18] Chauncey went on to found the Educational Testing Service, in 1947, which has inherited the College Board's role as administrator of the SAT (and has developed a host of popular graduate-level entrance exams in its own right).[19] By the 1950s, the College Board had grown to around three hundred members, and more than half a million students sat for the exam every year during that period.[20] Test-preparation companies, such as Kaplan and the Princeton Review, thrived as a result of the SAT's rise, and "much of the curriculum in American elementary and secondary education [was] reverse-engineered to raise SAT scores" to ensure admission to top universities.[21]

This leaves us in a particular quandary today, best described by Lucy Calkins, founding director of the Reading and Writing Project at Columbia University's Teachers College. Referring to the most recently appointed president of the College Board, she asks, "The issue is: Are we in a place to let Dave Coleman control the entire K–12 curriculum?"[22]

—m—

THIS IS NOT to say that the testocracy has continued to gain ground unabated. Close to eight hundred colleges have decreased or eliminated reliance on high-stakes tests as the way to rank and sort students. In the current environment, however, moving away from merit by the numbers takes guts. The testing and ranking diehards, intent on maintaining their gate-keeping role, hold back and even penalize administrators who take such measures. The presidents of both Reed College and Sarah Lawrence College report experiencing forms of retribution for refusing to cooperate with the "ranking roulette."[23]

At the center of this conflict is the wildly popular *US News & World Report*'s annual college-rankings issue—the bible of university prestige. In the book *Crazy U*, Andrew Ferguson describes meeting Bob Morse, the director of data research for *US News* and the lead figure behind the publication's college rankings. Morse, a small man who works in an unassuming office, is described by Ferguson as "the most powerful man in America."[24] And for good reason: students and parents often rely upon the rankings—reportedly produced only by Morse and a handful of other writers and editors[25]—as a proxy for university quality. These rankings rely heavily on SAT scores for their calculations. Without such data available from, for example, Sarah Lawrence, which stopped using SAT scores in its admissions process in 2005, Morse calculated Sarah Lawrence's ranking by assuming an average SAT score roughly 200 points below the average score of its peer group. How does *US News* justify simply making up a number? Michele Tolela Myers, the president of Sarah Lawrence at the time the school stopped using the SAT, reported that the reasoning behind the lowered ranking was explained to her this way: "[Director Morse] made it clear to me that he believes that schools that do not use SAT scores in their admission process are admitting less capable students and therefore should lose points on their selectivity index."[26]

This is the testocracy in action, an aristocracy determined by testing that wants to maintain its position even if it has to resort to fabrication.

What is it they are so desperate to protect? The answer initially seems to be that the SAT can predict how well students will do in college and thus how well-prepared they are to enter a particular school. There is a relationship between a student's SAT score and his first-year college grades. The problem is it's a very modest relationship. It is a positive relationship, meaning it is more than zero. But it is not what most people would assume when they hear the term *correlation*.

In 2004, economist Jesse Rothstein published an independent study that found only a meager 2.7 percent of grade variance in the first year of college can be effectively predicted by the SAT.[27] The LSAT has a similarly weak correlation to actual achievement in law school. Jane Balin, Michelle Fine, and I did a study at the University of Pennsylvania Law School, where we looked at the first-year law school grades of 981 students over several years and then looked at their LSAT scores. It turned out that there was a modest relationship between their test scores and their grades. The LSAT predicted 14 percent of the variance between the first-year grades. And it did a little better the second year: 15 percent. Which means that 85 percent of the time it was wrong. I remember being at a meeting with a person who at the time worked for the Law School Admission Council, which constructs the LSAT. When I brought these numbers up to her she actually seemed surprised they were that high. "Well," she said, "nationwide the test is nine percent better than random." Nine percent better than random. That's what we're talking about.

So, if the SAT does not correlate with the grades a student will get in college, how can a student's performance in college be predicted? William C. Hiss and Valerie W. Franks, both formerly of the Bates College admissions department, released a report in 2014 that studied thirty-three colleges and universities that required neither the SAT nor its very popular competitor the ACT for admission.[28] Now, which students did or did not choose to submit their standardized-test scores is in itself interesting—overwhelmingly those students who did not submit a score were women, minority students, or those who would be the first in their family to go to college, which should tell us a lot about the SAT right there.

In reviewing the performance of more than eighty-eight thousand students, Hiss and Franks found that students who perform well in college were the ones who had gotten strong grades in high school, even if they had weak SAT scores. They also found that students with weaker high school grades did less well in college—even if they had stronger SAT scores.[29] Summing up their findings they wrote, "Many of us who have spent our careers as secondary and university faculty and administrators find compelling the argument that 'what students do over four years in high school is more important than what they do on a Saturday morning.'"[30]

So, if the SAT does not measure aptitude—and if it doesn't even pretend to measure achievement—then what does it measure? I have argued for years that the SAT is actually more reliable as a "wealth test" than a test of potential, and the most recent results bear this out. Below are figures released in 2013[31] by the College Board that correlate SAT scores with the family income of the test taker.[32]

FAMILY INCOME	AVERAGE SAT SCORE (OUT OF 2400) FOR 2013 COLLEGE-BOUND SENIORS
$0,000–$20,000	1326
$20,000–$40,000	1402
$40,000–$60,000	1461
$60,000–$80,000	1497
$80,000–$100,000	1535
$100,000–$120,000	1569
$120,000–$140,000	1581
$140,000–$160,000	1604
$160,000–$200,000	1625
More than $200,000	1714

Now that is a correlation! This is what I refer to as the "Volvo effect." In *Crazy U*, Ferguson talks about how the parents of his son's friends and classmates were spending $30,000 to $35,000 to prepare their children for college. That isn't the amount they had to pay for a premier boarding school mind you—that was the amount they paid to hire someone to tutor their child on the SAT and to help them write their "statement of interest" essays on their college applications. When these students get in to a particular college we say that this process reflects the fairness of the meritocracy, but really it only reflects the fact that the elite dominate the entry to higher education. These students aren't smarter than the other students. Or to put it another way: they may be smart, but they are not necessarily those most likely to contribute to our society; they simply come from families that have more money to pay people to prepare them for the SAT, to test-prep them for their high school grades, and to pay for viola lessons so they can stand out more in the admissions process.

The SAT's most reliable value is its proxy for wealth. It is normed to white, upper-middle-class performance, as numerous studies have shown when the test is viewed through the lenses of race and class.[33] The figures below, from 2013, show this in stark relief.[34]

TEST-TAKER ETHNICITY	AVERAGE SAT SCORE (OUT OF 2400) FOR 2013 COLLEGE-BOUND SENIORS
Black or African American	1278
Mexican or Mexican American	1354
Puerto Rican	1354
Other Hispanic, Latino, or Latin American	1355
American Indian, Alaska Native	1427
Other	1501
White	1576
Asian, Asian American, Pacific Islander	1645

Is this a case of merit belonging to one race and not to another? Or is it the case that if you have grown up in a particular environment, such as one where your parents lack the funds to prepare you for these standardized tests or lack an advanced level of education themselves, you will not do as well on the SAT? There are other reasons why students of various ethnicities may underperform on the SAT. One of these is a phenomenon called "stereotype threat," a term coined by Claude Steele of Stanford University (now provost of the University of California at Berkeley) to describe the anxiety a person may experience when he or she has the potential to confirm a negative stereotype about his or her social group. Many first- and second-generation immigrants of color test well, for example, because they retain a national identity free of America's racial caste system and enjoy material and cultural advantages, including professional or well-educated parents. They do not internalize the stigma of race and are thus less affected by the anxiety of confirming assumptions of intellectual inferiority that depresses test scores of highly motivated students who are African American, Mexican American, or of Puerto Rican heritage.

I know this threat is real. One summer not too long ago, I was engaged in a long-term writing project and recruited an absolutely brilliant young man who is Latino. Enrique (not his real name) has a photographic memory. I mean, he blew my mind. I have never seen anybody who could tell you, "Oh, well that's on page 384. It's in the middle of the page. I think it's the first paragraph, not the second one." But Enrique could not do well on the LSAT, though he practiced taking it close to thirty times. Enrique grew up in a low-income community, so arguably that had something to do with the verbal references that he might have missed. But a lot more of it had to do with stereotype threat: he was too tense. Postscript to this story: Enrique was subsequently selected to be a Rhodes scholar. So what, really, are we talking about here?

If we can agree that the SAT, LSAT, and other standardized tests most reliably measure a student's household income, ethnicity, and level of parental education, then we can see that reliance on such test scores narrows the student body to those who come from particular house-holds. Then we must decide how to ensure that we open the admis-sions doors to a greater diversity of students—not just the ones from privileged backgrounds. I want to make it clear that I am not talking about affirmative action here. The loud debate over affirmative action is a distraction that obscures the real problem, because right now affir-mative action simply mirrors the values of the current view of meritoc-racy. Students at elite colleges, for example, who are the beneficiaries of affirmative action tend to be either the children of immigrants or the children of upper-middle-class parents of color who have been sent to fine prep schools just like the upper-middle-class white students. The result? Our nation's colleges, universities, and graduate schools use affirmative-action-based practices to admit students who test well, and then they pride themselves on their cosmetic diversity. Thus, affirma-tive action has evolved in many (but not all) colleges to merely mimic elite-sponsored admissions practices that transform wealth into merit, encourage over-reliance on pseudoscientific measures of excellence, and convert admission into an entitlement without social obligation.

No, the question, as I said in the previous chapter, is this: How do we move from admission to mission? Further: How do we move past that moment of admission, which may only confirm one's present sta-tus, to granting an opportunity for a diverse and worthy group of in-dividuals to learn how to work together collectively and/or creatively to help solve the deep challenges confronting our communities, our economy, and our educational experiences in a democratic society? Of course, some of this has to do with how we define success. A study of Harvard alumni over three decades, which culminated in the 1990s, defined "success" by income, community involvement, and professional satisfaction.[35] Researchers found a high correlation between those cri-teria and two criteria that might not ordinarily be associated with Har-vard freshmen: low SAT scores and a blue-collar background. This is echoed by college admissions officers at elite universities today, who re-port—when asked what predicts life success—that, above a minimum level of competence, "initiative" or "hunger" are the best predictors. Marlyn McGrath Lewis, director of admissions for Harvard, says, "We have particular interest in students from a modest background. Coupled with high achievement and a high ambition level and energy, a background that's modest can really be a help. We know that's the best investment we can make: a kid who's hungry."[36] That's certainly the message of Derek Bok and William Bowen's *The Shape of the River*, that those who are motivated to take advantage of an opportunity, when given the opportunity, can and often do succeed, often in ways that are different than their more privileged peers. The African American students in the Bok-Bowen study, for example, became leaders within their communities at much higher rates than their more affluent and better-scoring white counterparts.

When I speak here of diversity, I'm not talking strictly along color or gender lines either. When the GI Bill was first proposed, toward the end of World War II, some university officials did their best to get it defeated. They were appalled by the prospect of what they saw as a mob of unprepared, unsuitable men trying to be their students. To their surprise, the veterans—many of them poor, most the first in their families to attend college—proved to be among the best students of their generation. By broadening access to college for those who had served their country, the GI Bill helped fuel the post–World War II economic boom while leveling the playing field for many Americans. The bill epitomized our country's dual commitments: to open opportunity across the economic spectrum and to invest in people who will give back to society.

We see the problem of restricted access today in the new elite class, which passes on its privileges in the same way that the old elite from twentieth-century America passed on its privileges. But there is an even more worrisome aspect of the new elite. The old elite felt that it had inherited its privileges; in order to defend the social oligarchy over which it reigned, the old elite felt the need to give back through public service or a financial commitment to the greater good. The old elite recognized that it had been privileged by the accident of birth, so the message to those who were out of luck was that you were unfortunate but it was through no defect of your own.

The new elite, on the other hand, feels that it has earned its privileges based on intrinsic, individual merit. The message, therefore, to those who are not part of this elite is "You are stupid. You simply don't matter. I deserve all the advantages I'm granted." This attitude manifests in the jobs that college grads now take. For example, the student-run *Harvard Crimson* ran an article in 2007 about that year's graduating class smirking that "only" 43 percent of female graduates entered finance and consulting compared to 58 percent of male graduates.[37] The article, entitled "'07 Men Make More," explained—with apparent disdain—that women choose jobs in lower-paying fields such as education and public service.[38]

Despite the economic downturn of recent years, the striking number of Harvard graduates entering finance and consulting has persisted. The class of 2013 senior survey showed that more than 30 percent of the 2013 class had jobs in those fields.[39] After consulting and finance, the technology/engineering industry captured 13 percent of Harvard graduates that year. The *Crimson* again emphasized—with what seems to me to be the appearance of similar disdain—the preference of women to pursue less-lucrative work in education, media, and health care rather than in finance, consulting, and technology.[40]

The top career choices of many male Harvard students—whether it is 2007 or 2013—are severely lacking in any element of service. This is the damage that we are doing through our testocracy. We are credentializing a new elite by legitimizing people with an inflated sense of their own merit and little unwillingness to open up to new ways of problem solving. They exude an arrogance that says there's only one way to answer a question—because the SAT only gives credit for the one right answer.

The world, by contrast, provides us with more than one correct answer to most questions. In the face of mounting criticism, the College Board has recently proposed changes to the SAT, including reducing the use of obscure vocabulary words, narrowing the areas from which the math questions will be drawn, and making the essay section optional.

But individuals such as Bard College president Leon Botstein find these proposed changes are too little, too late because they don't address the test's real problem. In an eloquent rebuttal, Botstein writes:

> The essential mechanism of the SAT, the multiple choice question, is a bizarre relic of long outdated twentieth century social scientific assumptions and strategies. As every adult recognizes, knowing something or how to do something in real life is never defined by being able to choose a "right" answer from a set of possible answers (some of them intentionally misleading). . . . No scientist, engineer, writer, psychologist, artist, or physician—and certainly no scholar, and therefore no serious university faculty member—pursues his or her vocation by getting right answers from a set of prescribed alternatives that trivialize complexity and ambiguity.[41]

Meaningful participation in a democratic society depends upon citizens who are willing to develop and utilize these three skills: collaborative problem solving, independent thinking, and creative leadership. But these skills bear no relationship to success in the testocracy. Aptitude tests do not predict leadership, emotional intelligence, or the capacity to work with others to contribute to society. All that a test like the SAT promises is a (very, very slight) correlation with first-year college grades.

But once you're past the first year or two of higher education, success isn't about being the best test taker in the room any longer. It's about being able to work with other people who have different strengths than you and who are also prepared to back you up when you make a mistake or when you feel vulnerable. Our colleges and universities have to take pride not in compiling an individualistic group of very-high-scoring students but in nurturing a diverse group of thinkers and facilitating how they solve complex problems creatively—because complex problems seem to be all the world has in store for us these days.

CHAPTER THREE

From Testocratic Merit to Democratic Merit

THE CURRENT MERITOCRACY—rule by testocratic merit—uses easily measurable criteria to award status to individuals. This efficiency is part of the testocracy's appeal. In the opinion of Bard College president Leon Botstein, this seeming objectivity is what has kept testocratic merit, as represented by success on the SAT, around so long:

> The real responsibility for our sorry state of affairs regarding college entrance examinations rests with our colleges and universities themselves. The elite institutions have willingly supported an alliance with the College Board to make their own lives easier, and we Americans seem to have accepted this owing to our misplaced love affair with standardized testing and rankings as the proper means to ensure educational excellence.[1]

As we shift our concept of merit from being a testable, rankable commodity for the few to a measure that might be reached by talented people of all social classes we have to ask ourselves: How shall we find the means to recognize and foster democratic merit? To answer this question we must first consider what the word "democratic" means and how a democracy truly functions. In a seminal 1997 article, David Labaree argued that the educational enterprise in America is instructed by three primary goals.[2] The first goal, "democratic equality," reflects society's interest both in creating an informed and engaged citizenry and in promoting relative equality. The second goal, "social efficiency," emphasizes the necessity in a market-based economy of having productive and innovative laborers. The third goal, "social mobility," treats education as a commodity whose sole purpose is to advance individual standing in the hierarchy of societal order. The first two goals further the public interest, while the third goal unquestionably characterizes education as a "private good," the virtues of which are "selective and differential rather than collective and equal."

Of course the third goal is what we have now, which is why, as Labaree points out, the acquisition of meaningless academic credentials (instead of socially valuable skills and knowledge) has become our paramount concern. He concludes that this problem can be fixed only by promoting the other two goals, democratic equality and social efficiency. Essentially, Labaree's findings illustrate that testocratic merit tends to maintain the status quo by placing a higher value on testing than on training, on aesthetics than on substance, on competition than on collaboration. If Labaree's thesis is correct—that is to say, if our society truly values education as a means to prepare citizens to participate in our democracy, to train workers, and to enable individuals to improve their lots—then we need a culture shift about how we reevaluate the meaning of merit by measuring its democratic values rather than its testocratic machinery.

Democratic merit makes different assumptions than testocratic merit. First, democratic merit is related to its context: it is a function of the goals and purposes (mission) of the institution that wants to use it as a metric of selection. There is no standard of merit that does not involve a choice about which characteristics of applicants are valuable. The measures for democratic merit you will read about in this book—peer collaboration, leadership, drive—all may take some getting used to. It will be important to remember that the current prevailing notion of merit in college admissions—as a function of standardized-test scores and secondary school grades—is neither objectively true nor natural.

The second assumption that democratic merit makes is that the purpose of colleges and universities has a public character. The vast majority of institutions of higher education say that directly in their "mission statements." Let's take them at their word then: democratic merit is the form of merit that views higher education, at least partially, as a public good. As such, admissions criteria should continuously be reassessed for the degree to which they help the institution and its constituents to make present and future contributions to society, that is, our democracy. Democratic merit does what our current meritocracy fails to do: it creates an incentive system that emphasizes the development of more and more individuals who serve the goals and contribute to the conditions of a thriving democracy for both their own good as well as for the collective good. Granting these individuals educational access, regardless of their supposed possession of abstractly measured "talent," is what will contribute to the creation of higher-level problem solving.

WHEN FUTURE SUPREME Court justice Sonia Sotomayor began college at Princeton, she felt entirely out of place. "I felt like an alien landing in another universe," she recounted in a recent speech to college alumni and reiterated in a rare oral dissent from the Supreme Court bench.[3] The Ivy League was certainly a long way from home; she had grown up in a Bronx housing project, suffering from diabetes and living with an alcoholic father.

Sotomayor's story of a young woman who beat the odds embodies the American Dream narrative. Despite the fact that in New York, as in the rest of the country, the academic success of a child is heavily determined by race and socioeconomic status,[4] Sotomayor went on to receive her law degree from Yale, work at the Manhattan district attorney's office, and ultimately be appointed to the highest court in the land.

Sotomayor's story of success, despite all expectations to the contrary, is as inspiring as it appeared rare to the white and wealthy students who were her classmates and who viewed only themselves as succeeding by traditional standards. Sotomayor recalls letters in the *Daily Princetonian* "lamenting the presence on campus of 'affirmative action students,' each of whom had presumably displaced a far more deserving affluent white male and could rightly be expected to crash into the gutter built of her own unrealistic aspirations."[5]

But this story of the American university as a place driven by competitive individualism and test scores, a place where students of color, poor students, and others unfavored by wealth-dependent standardized tests must face isolation and fatiguing odds, has not always been the singular story of the purpose and role of our institutions of higher education.

In the spring of 1968, after the assassination of Martin Luther King Jr., the Reverend John Brooks demonstrated a competing understanding of higher education when he drove up and down the eastern seaboard to hand select a number of African American men for admission to the College of the Holy Cross, including Clarence Thomas, as we saw in chapter 1. For Brooks, increasing access to higher education was a moral imperative, as well as a practical one: Holy Cross could not shape the nation's leaders when it neglected a generation of ambitious black men.[6]

Brooks drove south from Massachusetts, searching for young men who had ambition, leadership potential, and strong character rather than the right family pedigree or the right test scores. Brooks found the qualities he was searching for in a young man who was determined to become the first black priest in Savannah, Georgia; in another who had performed under pressure to elevate his basketball team to the state championship; and in still another whose "quiet intensity," molded by a childhood spent moving from one rat-infested place to another, spoke more to his character than his poor grades.

Brooks ultimately selected twenty black men: nineteen freshmen and one sophomore. The men started at Holy Cross in the fall of 1968, and during their years there, Brooks mentored them, affirming their potential and cultivating their merit rather than expecting their individual merit to arrive whole and intact.

When one student felt discouraged by his 2.3 grade point average, Brooks sent him a letter of praise and encouragement. By the end of the following semester, the student had earned a 3.2 GPA. Brooks provided eyeglasses for another student, which allowed the young man to improve his grades significantly. Brooks provided his students with supplies and transportation, as well as support at their football games and antiwar rallies.

When the students created the college's first-ever Black Student Union, Brooks listened to the goals they outlined in their first meeting, goals that included adding more black students and professors and including more black authors in the curriculum. Brooks then helped plan a dinner between the BSU and the university president so that the administration could learn of the students' struggles and of their ideas.

Brooks himself fought for the inclusion of black studies courses in the curriculum, and he successfully added the courses Black Literature and Perspectives on Racism. He also recruited black faculty, including Ogretta McNeil, who admired Brooks's single-handed attempt to integrate Holy Cross.

One of the most heated moments at Holy Cross occurred after the school's disciplinary board disproportionately suspended black student protesters, who had been offended by job recruiters who did not consider black applicants. In response, all the African American students staged a walkout, leaving Holy Cross the option to make a powerful statement against racism. Brooks respected the students' unanimous choice to walk out, and he insisted that he would work with the school administration to remedy the situation. Brooks approached the president of Holy Cross and said flatly, "There are times when one principle has to override another." Brooks worked around the clock to bring together a council, which included a respected black community activist, so that the president could reconsider the facts of the case. Meanwhile, Brooks gave a couple of hundred dollar bills to the black students, who were now living off campus; he wanted to ensure that the students could eat since they no longer had access to the campus cafeteria.

The council meeting with the president grew increasingly heated as faculty members spoke up against special treatment for black students. Brooks listened to the discussion, and during breaks in the meeting, he updated the black students as to what was happening. After a weekend of listening to various perspectives of the student protest and subsequent disciplinary measures, the president granted amnesty to the suspended students. In response, the black students agreed to return to school. At the conclusion of this ordeal, Brooks was seen with tears in his eyes.

Father Brooks never gave up on these twenty black men, and he provided them with unwavering support throughout their time at Holy Cross. He cultivated the potential he saw in each man, guiding them as they were challenged academically, shaped socially, and strengthened by the racial isolation that defined their campus and the racial tumult that defined their country.

Brooks's students eventually graduated from Holy Cross and went off to storied careers. Among the twenty men are Clarence Thomas, associate justice of the US Supreme Court; Edward P. Jones, Pulitzer Prize winner; Theodore Wells, renowned defense attorney; and Stanley Grayson, former deputy mayor of New York and president of M. R. Beal & Company, one of the country's oldest black-owned investment banks. Even today, decades after their graduation, the men attribute their success to Father Brooks. According to Grayson, without Father Brooks, "none of us would have made it."

Brooks had seen in each of the men characteristics of value and potential for greatness that could not be assessed by tests alone. As the men faced the academic and social challenges of higher education, the color of their skin, the diversity of their backgrounds, and the untraditional metrics of their aptitude did not prove to be obstacles that left them, as Justice Sotomayor's Princeton classmates might have expected, flailing under their unrealistic aspirations. Rather, with Brooks's unwavering mentorship, each man's democratic merit was forged.

I mentioned earlier that this book is not about affirmative action. That statement needs to be qualified. It is not about an affirmative action that refuses to challenge the current meritocracy but instead simply adapts, so that at the moment of admissions, a few students of color are selected and the burden is then placed on them to assimilate. It is not about an affirmative action that relieves universities of their responsibility to mentor and nurture their students. It is not about an affirmative action that wrongly holds at fault its so-called beneficiaries for the fundamental flaws of our test-driven merit system. Indeed, where affirmative action has failed, it has failed because it has not gone far enough to address the unfairness of both our current merit system and its wealth-driven definition of merit. However, when we redefine merit by those characteristics that indicate a student's potential for future success in our democracy—leadership, the ability to collaborate with others, resiliency, and a drive to learn, among others—then we might be able to make use of actions that prioritize such traits. If we commit to mentoring and nurturing that potential in our students, universities might more successfully cultivate potential leaders as Father Brooks did.

"YOU DO NOT take a person who, for years, has been hobbled by chains and liberate him, bring him up to the starting line of a race and then say, 'You are free to compete with all the others,' and still justly believe that you have been completely fair.[7] President Lyndon B. Johnson used these words to lay the foundation for affirmative action in his 1965 commencement speech at Howard University. Johnson believed that equal opportunity was essential but not enough. Though all people are born with a similar range of abilities, ability "is stretched or stunted by the family that you live with, the neighborhood you live in—by the school you go to and the poverty or the richness of your surroundings." President Johnson proposed affirmative action to ensure that black students therefore might "have the ability to walk through those gates" of equal opportunity.

Following his commencement address, in 1965 President Johnson issued Executive Order 11246, which required federal contractors, including public universities, to take affirmative action to promote the full realization of equal opportunities for women and people of color.[8] Throughout the nation, university admission policies began to take race into account, allowing students of color a "tip factor" in admissions.[9] At elite universities, admissions officers began to rely on the university's authority to create a student body consistent with their educational missions.[10]

Affirmative action came under siege in June 1974, when Allan Bakke filed suit after being denied admission to the University of California at Davis Medical School. Bakke claimed that UC Davis's policy of reserving 16 percent of the class for students of color denied white applicants like him equal protection of law.[11] UC Davis Medical School, like many universities, justified affirmative action as necessary to produce diversity.[12] In his suit, Bakke challenged both the goal of diversity and the manner in which the university achieved it.

For more than eight months, universities waited to hear back from the Supreme Court, worried about the threat the case posed to "the autonomy traditionally granted universities and their faculties in making admissions decisions."[13] When the Court finally issued an opinion on *Regents of the University of California v. Bakke*, the universities breathed a sigh of relief. Writing for the Court, Justice Lewis Powell Jr. had bridged the conservative desire to end affirmative action and the liberal acknowledgment of past purposeful discrimination.[14] The opinion declared that the medical school's racial quota violated equal protection, but much to the relief of university deans of admissions, the Court did not prohibit UC Davis from using race as a potential factor in admissions.[15]

Instead, Powell's opinion affirmed the academic goal of racial diversity, writing that admissions policies may consider race to "obtain . . . the educational benefits that flow from an ethnically diverse student body."[16] An applicant's race could be a factor in admissions decisions because diversity represented a "compelling state interest."[17]

At Harvard, not only did the elite university rest assured that its control over its own admissions process was still intact; it was delighted to find that Justice Powell praised their school, which, unlike UC Davis, still required applicants of color to compete with all the other applicants for available spots.[18] Powell's opinion affirmed the use of race, as well as other factors such as geography and "life spent on a farm," as a "plus" factor in admissions.[19] The Court applauded such a policy as being "flexible enough to consider all pertinent elements of diversity in light of the particular qualifications of each applicant, and to place them on the same footing for consideration, although not necessarily according them the same weight."[20]

As we saw in chapter 1, the Supreme Court again upheld race-conscious admissions policies in the 2003 case, *Grutter v. Bollinger*. Grutter had argued that the university had discriminated against her on the basis of her race when it had rejected her under an admissions policy that allowed consideration of race to be a potential factor in admissions. But the Supreme Court once again held, in an opinion written by Justice Sandra Day O'Connor, that the appropriate use of race in university admissions was justified and found that "student body diversity is a compelling state interest."[21]

In doing so, the Court affirmed that the democratic mission of higher education is to train a range of future leaders who are representative of our heterogeneous society. In the years following *Grutter*, the idea of diversity gained important traction in our culture, becoming a fundamental part of understanding what it means to live in a democracy. It was also met with vehement backlash, as the Allan Bakkes and Barbara Grutters of a demographically changing America felt their coveted spots at elite institutions increasingly threatened by the access that affirmative action gave to those populations who historically had been kept from competing for them. Opponents of affirmative action have derided the currently admitted "diverse" student pool as less deserving than white students. Like Justice Sotomayor's classmates who wrote to the *Daily Princetonian*, these opponents perceive the lower standardized-test scores of students of color to be indicators that these students have bypassed "fair and square" competition.

The conservative opposition has even argued that affirmative action in fact hurts those it is supposed to help by lowering admission standards, admitting black students and other students of color to universities on account of their race instead of on their merit (meaning their testocratic merit, I am sure). According to these critics, once the students of color are admitted, the programs prove too difficult for them, and they perform badly.[22] Underperformance then further results in "disidentification with academic excellence" and "low effort syndrome."[23] According to Abigail and Stephen Thernstrom and their colleagues, affirmative action creates "disincentives for black and Latino students to work hard by creating expectations among such students that they will benefit from preferential treatment on the basis of race in the future."[24]

IN JUNE 2013, the Supreme Court again addressed affirmative action in the case I discussed earlier, *Fisher v. University of Texas*, which was brought by a white student, Abigail Fisher, who was denied admission to the University of Texas at Austin.[25] Like Allan Bakke and Barbara Grutter before her, Fisher charged that the university's admission process unfairly discriminated against her as a white student.

Fisher charged that race should not be considered as one factor among many others, including letters of recommendation, personal essays, and socioeconomic background. In bringing the suit, Fisher said she hoped the Supreme Court would "completely take race out of the issue in terms of admissions and that everyone will be able to get into any school that they want no matter what race they are but solely based on their merit and if they work hard for it."[26]

Fisher and other opponents of affirmative action single out race as an admissions criterion—before musical ability, athletic accomplishment, or any other factor—because race is seen as undeserving of consideration in a holistic admissions review.[27] Opponents also imagine that a student's merit can be measured, identified, standardized, and divorced from the context of a student's race, a claim that is in direct contrast to the stated mission of the UT system:

> To provide superior, accessible, affordable instruction and learning opportunities to undergraduate, graduate, and professional school students from a wide range of social, ethnic, cultural, and economic backgrounds, thereby preparing educated, productive citizens who can meet the rigorous challenges of an increasingly diverse society and an ever-changing global community.[28]

In its much-anticipated *Fisher* opinion, the Supreme Court did not end affirmative action. But the UT admissions system, which considers race as one factor among many, is now at risk again. Fisher and her supporters may prevail in their crusade to eliminate race in UT's consideration of its next class of students. They may reduce UT's admissions process to a sterile measure of an individual's test scores and grades. In doing so, they ignore what Father Brooks knew about his twenty young recruits: the story of any individual's potential is told both in the context of race and class, as well as the important role of mentorship and the ability to work together, among other non-testable, non-quantifiable factors. As Father Brooks discovered, it is in the context of race that a young boy might first consider ambitions of being the first black priest of a southern town. Or another might, while surviving a childhood of poverty and insecurity, develop the strong character and resilience that will one day make a powerful leader.

What's more, Fisher and critics of affirmative action dismiss the important benefits that diversity provides for all students on college campuses. For the educational institutions in our democracy to be spaces of better deliberation for all of us, they must become more diverse and inclusive. In Justice Sotomayor's case, her background as a Latina and woman of color, as well as her childhood of economic struggle in the Bronx, enabled her to contribute important insights to the jurisprudence of the Court. In fact, if the half-century-long experiment in affirmative action has given us a glimpse of anything, it is into how important diversity is to the way people think, talk, and work with one another, particularly in our institutions of higher education. The most recent social science research and the lived experience of hundreds of thousands of students have taught us that meaningful diversity can be an active, if not essential, ingredient in the production of our best work as individuals and in groups.

Racial diversity empowers those with dissenting opinions to speak up. One study found that groups that are more diverse provide a more comfortable, safe space for dissenting members—of all backgrounds—to voice their differing opinions. These perspectives then lead to increased divergent thinking and perspective-taking by the group as a whole.[29] Women have also been shown to speak up more when they are in racially diverse groups than when in all-white ones.[30]

Overall group performance, as well as the performance of white participants in particular, also benefits from diversity. Research has shown that racially diverse pairs of people are more task-focused and engage in a more detailed, in-depth, and accurate discussion with their partner than non-diverse pairs.[31] The complexity of conversation increases when a group includes people of color and when group members report having racially diverse friends and classmates.[32]

Research has also shown that white participants make fewer factual errors when working with a racially mixed group.[33] In one study, participants were asked to sit through a simulated trial as members of the jury. Some of the juries were all white, while others were racially diverse, containing four white and two black jurors. The juries' deliberation sessions were videotaped, and researchers found in studying the sessions that the racially diverse juries deliberated longer and considered a wider range of information than the all-white juries did. What is more, it was the white participants who were largely responsible for this difference: they raised more case facts, made fewer factual errors, and were more amenable to discussion of race-related issues than their peers in all-white juries.

Similar findings have been made in classroom settings. One study found that white students are more likely to read more carefully and retain more information when they are aware they will be discussing their readings in a racially diverse setting than when they believe they will be doing so in an all-white setting.[34] Another study found that white college students who are assigned non-white roommates are less anxious, more natural, and less verbally controversial when meeting a person of color for the first time than are white students who have white roommates.[35]

True diversity that brings together a group of individuals more representative of the world we live in can help all of us rethink tasks, synthesize information better, and innovate creative ways to solve problems. Yet there are those who attack affirmative action as going too far to provide "unmerited" access to higher education for students of color at the expense of "deserving" applicants. However, the research and the lived experiences of these students would suggest that mere cosmetic diversity in fact does not go far enough.

Justice Sotomayor's story provides an example of how affirmative action does not go far enough. She was one of a handful of people of color admitted to Princeton, where she initially struggled academically but later flourished. Her success is surely a testament to her character, but she was one of the lucky few admitted into Princeton through a narrow affirmative action policy. While Justice Sotomayor's story proves that when students of color get into universities, they can thrive and become successful, the rarity of stories like hers also sounds a warning bell that affirmative action is not going far enough.

When setting out to recruit students for Holy Cross, Father Brooks rejected a test-based meritocracy, recognizing both that a student's potential was not summed up in a simple test score and, even more important, that the university needed to play an active role in mentoring and cultivating students' potential once they arrived on campus. By contrast, affirmative action as it is now practiced leaves in place the underlying values of the current testocracy, creating only a small opening for a select few students of color. As a result, those individuals who benefit from affirmative action are seen by some as undeserving and illegitimate and not meritorious.

The criticism that says undeserving students of color use affirmative action to cheat the meritocratic system is therefore problematic and circular. It blames the canaries for the poisonous air in the defective mine we have built.[36] In the defective, poisonous mine that is our current meritocracy, "merit" is defined by a set of characteristics that primarily mirror wealth. And affirmative action adapts to and operates within this meritocracy without disturbing its fundamental assumptions.

Thus, affirmative action invariably replicates test-score-driven, individualized competition among students of color. For example, elite institutions often compete among themselves for the small pool of candidates of color who are "adequately prepared" to succeed at top universities, which excludes many who could perform well academically in college if they, like the mentees of Father Brooks, receive unwavering support and encouragement.[37] Instead of providing presently disadvantaged African American students thoroughgoing access to higher education and genuine opportunities to have mentors and peers who nurture and reinforce their potential, many institutions simply achieve their stated goals of "diversity" by admitting black students from high-income families, first- and second-generation black immigrants from Africa and the Caribbean, and biracial students who may not even identify as "black."[38]

Aisha Haynie noticed this phenomenon when she attended Harvard College between 1996 and 2000. She discovered that when she told her fellow black classmates that she was not from the West Indies or Africa but from the Carolinas, they would say, "No, where are you really from?"[39] Prompted by these experiences, Haynie wrote and later published a senior honors thesis on the origins and ancestry of Harvard's black students. She found that though Harvard—like many other elite institutions—had seen and celebrated the increasing enrollment of black students, in fact, African American students continued to be underrepresented, particularly those who were descended from multiple generations of American forebears, including the descendants of slaves and particularly those from the American South.[40] This is significant because Caribbean, African, and other biracial or bi-ethnic students had different perceptions of their own identity within the American social context.[41] What is more, West Indian students' parents were better off than the families of black American students, and more than 90 percent of the parents of Harvard's African students had advanced degrees.[42]

Though Haynie's study should not be misread as discounting the value that Caribbean and African immigrant students bring to a college campus, it says important things about the ways in which affirmative action is not enough, by itself, to provide meaningful access to higher education, in this case to poor and working-class American descendants of slaves: a group of African American students who would likely thrive at college—if our institutions were not so singularly focused on test-based admissions.

JUSTICE THOMAS NOW argues that affirmative action is wrong. In a peculiar sense, he is right—but for the wrong reason. If affirmative action has failed, it's not because it has admitted unmeritorious students of color at the expense of whites, or that it has failed to propel us into a postracial, color-blind society. Rather, affirmative action's weakness and vulnerability cooperate with, and perhaps unintentionally legitimate, a meritocracy that privileges test scores over other indicators of student potential in the first place. Affirmative action has fed into the societal vision we have of our citizens belonging to their place in a pyramid—some further up, some further down—our positions based to some degree on where we were born or on how successfully we have clawed our way up over others. What we need in order to switch to democratic merit is to topple this pyramid onto its side and flatten it out into an oval—the best visual representation for our democratic society going forward.

It is always challenging to unseat a paradigm. And yet it should alarm us all that today few shelves at Barnes and Nobles are dedicated to students' academic development during college, while rows and rows offer books of test preparation and essay-writing tips for college applicants. Parents can pay $40,000 a year to hire independent college admissions counselors who advise high school students and guide them into the Ivy League. The emphasis—and money—placed on demonstrating "merit" on applications, rather than on nurturing a student's potential during the college years, results in institutions that lack meaningful race and class diversity. Simultaneously, these institutions may also fail not only in developing potential civic leadership with roots in democratizing merit for We the People, not just for We the Self-Appointed Leaders of Tomorrow.

In our admissions-obsessed college culture, institutions of higher education too often fail to prioritize their Father Brooks–like role of mentoring and nurturing student potential after admission. But a growing body of strong social science research lays bare the need for a culture shift in our meritocracy. This research explains why it no longer makes sense to define "merit" as race-blind, individualized, and test-score driven. We understand better now how meaningful diversity, as discussed in this chapter, benefits us all. And we know that we must fundamentally redefine "merit" to reflect the valuable work that diversity does for all individuals within a group.

If our higher education system is to remain competitive in the global information economy of the twenty-first century, we will have to move toward creating campuses where students live with other-race peers, have meaningful conversations with classmates with different perspectives, and are therefore pushed to be more thoughtful about our collective history and our democracy. To do so requires that we rethink our meritocracy and our definition of "merit" altogether. This shift may appear revolutionary, but there are already educational institutions, academic thought, and practical implications of democratic merit emerging and even thriving within today's testocracy.

There is the University Park Campus School in the Main South neighborhood of Worcester, Massachusetts. While many schools direct educators to "teach to the test" and emphasize rote memorization in their lesson plans, UPCS, a public charter school for grades seven through twelve, advocates a "thinking curriculum" that encourages student writing and rewards the expression of independent opinion. At UPCS, there are no placement tests or alternative tracks for different-level learners, and teachers and parents are jointly invested in the raising-up of the city's youth. As a result, UPCS's attendance rate hovers near 100 percent, whereas the number of dropouts, suspensions, and expulsions has fallen to zero.[43] The school's enthusiasm has rippled beyond its four walls and into the community itself, lifting it from decades of blight.

About an hour drive east of UPCS, in a physics classroom at Harvard College, the same critical thinking is taking place. In Professor Eric Mazur's introductory physics class, the students are fully engaged in their own learning. Unlike most college classes where the professor lectures for the entire period, in Mazur's class, the students engage in peer instruction, debating in pairs and attempting to reach a consensus on a response to Mazur's physics problems. Through this collaboration, the students—as well as Mazur—have found they learn better.

In a college classroom across the country, another professor has also shifted toward collaboration. Uri Treisman, then a graduate student at the University of California at Berkeley, redesigned his calculus curriculum to emphasize peer teamwork, social support networks, and higher-level problem solving. He found that students who struggled in his calculus class were those who studied alone. Thus, he created a curriculum that required students to work with their peers and create a community based on giving and receiving help. As with UPCS and Mazur's physics class, Treisman's students thrived when encouraged to collaborate.

UPCS, Mazur, and Treisman are not mere aberrations but rather three examples of the transformation occurring in education. There are also others offering alternatives to the traditional test-based understanding of merit: New York City's Vanguard High School, which replaced standardized testing with portfolio assessments; The Posse Foundation, which admits budding scholars based on character traits like teamwork, rather than on grades; the Mayo Clinic, which offers better health-care outcomes because its doctors solve problems collectively. I'm going to turn now to explore these and other examples that will demonstrate the benefits of a much-needed sea change in our understanding of "merit," as well as blueprints for making that a more far-reaching reality.

PART II
THE SOLUTION/S

CHAPTER FOUR

Taking Down Fences at University Park Campus School

THE SOLUTIONS TO the problem of testocratic merit are already in our midst. You know you are among them when you walk down the halls of a preparatory high school and the prevailing mood is one of cheerfulness. Everyone is in a good mood at University Park Campus School in Worcester; there isn't a sense of danger or of people competing with each other. Students who are having trouble with certain issues will just ask somebody, "Can you help me with this?" Such collaboration fosters a near 100 percent graduation rate and a near 100 percent matriculation rate at four-year colleges in a neighborhood where such statistics are unheard of. This is what comes from an interactive and responsive approach that develops a way to work with other people who have different strengths. The story of how this school came to be is nothing short of inspiring.

IN THE MID-1980S, administrators at Clark University, also in Worcester, Massachusetts, knew they had a problem. Prospective students and faculty were deterred by the high-poverty, high-crime area surrounding its campus. Marked by deteriorating and abandoned buildings, gangs, and drug trafficking, the Main South neighborhood was slipping into what some described as a state of abject disrepair. Deanna Leite, a local student, describes a murder that took place across the street from her house, recalling, "When I grew up, I wasn't allowed to cross the street."

Several years later, however, Deanna was attending the University Park Campus School, the centerpiece of an urban renewal program that brought world-class educational opportunities to this once-deteriorating neighborhood. Kelleigh Surrette, whose family has battled joblessness, homelessness, mental illness, and drug addiction, enrolled her ten children at UPCS. After graduation, her eldest son entered Middlebury College, and her eldest daughter went to Clark University for free, a benefit of attending UPCS. One of Kelleigh's younger daughters, who suffered from auditory perception problems and did not speak until she was four, starred in high school plays at UPCS. Kelleigh never attended college, but after seeing her kids' academic achievement, she resolved to go back to school to become a teacher. "This is more than a school," she said of UPCS. "It's a community."

The community Kelleigh describes grew out of "enlightened self-interest," as Thomas Del Prete put it. Del Prete, director of the Jacob Hiatt Center for Urban Education at Clark, said the university "realized that its own future was at stake."

The town-and-gown divide in Worcester was not so easily bridged, however. Initially, Clark wanted to put even more distance between itself and the encroaching urban blight. According to Jack Foley, vice president for Government and Community Affairs and Campus Services at Clark, the university thought its options were either to put up higher walls or move. "But to ignore your neighborhood is hypocritical. You can't do that," Foley concluded. "You've got to take fences down and strengthen your neighborhood."

Clark officials began by donating to local causes that would benefit both the neighborhood and the school. The question for all involved was, as Foley recalls, "How do we strengthen our future?" They created the University Park Partnership, made up of residents, businesspeople, clergy, and school and local government officials.

Incorporated as the Main South Community Development Corporation, the concerned parties began to make various improvements to the neighborhood. The university took an active but collaborative role, holding just one of fifteen seats on the board of directors. Foley describes how ceding control to the partnership was key to its success. "Long-term sustainable change will only happen if all the members of the community are making decisions," he observes.

The corporation's first step, from 1986 to 1995, was to create affordable housing from the many abandoned-property units in the area. The buildings were renovated by 1994; however, the crime and poverty persisted.

At a loss for how to proceed, Foley and others at Clark tried putting themselves in the shoes of local residents. "What would it take for us to live in this neighborhood?" they asked. Then they worked with the partnership to draw up a list of desirable qualities for a residential neighborhood and set about creating a plan for attaining them. The list included building and infrastructure rehabilitation, public safety, economic development, social and recreational programs, and education.

To begin, Clark opened its doors to local students, providing free tuition to any student living within eight blocks of the university (the poor Main South neighborhood that the community plan was designed to improve), provided they gained admission to Clark through regular application. Foley explained that the goal was to make college a real option for students who succeed academically, despite coming from extremely disadvantaged backgrounds. "College is foreign to these kids," he said of the Main South students. "They think it's for rich kids." The free tuition was designed to change that mind-set.

In return, Clark not only benefited from community growth—by adding to the value of the residential neighborhood the possibility of free college tuition—but it diversified its student body without altering any admissions criteria. There was no added cost to the university, either, as Clark was able to finance the free tuition by redirecting existing financial aid dollars toward these students, all of whom qualified for financial aid.

However, this neighborhood perk remained just that. Clark's charitable contribution to a select few neighborhood kids did not transform the community in any meaningful way. Since Clark maintained the same admissions criteria for its local students as for all others, it was merely offering financial aid to a few underprivileged families, rather than expanding educational opportunities for all the underprivileged students in the area.

Clearly more was needed to improve the futures of the Main South youth. The partnership concluded that a school could serve as "the centerpiece for neighborhood stability," as Del Prete described. So in 1997, they founded University Park Campus School, a full college-preparatory program that would admit students by lottery. The university offered $390,000 from a federal grant, Clark faculty and tutors, and access to Clark classes and facilities. The city provided the school building and agreed to pay for building maintenance, salaries, and supplies.

The president of Clark at the time, Richard P. Traina, explained the thinking behind the school: "If this neighborhood is to be revitalized, if it's to be a genuine community, the young people need to have hope. This is part of that plan by trying to provide them the very best education that we can manage with the initiatives from the school system and the help Clark University can provide."

As part of this collaboration, Clark master's degree candidates and undergraduates can complete work-study requirements by tutoring local students after school. UPCS teachers coteach professional development courses with Clark faculty during the summer, providing them free to teachers at Worcester public schools. In addition, UPCS teachers and Clark professors often teach together or teach one another's classes.

The local school ultimately serves as a clinical-training site for the university's teacher preparation program, with opportunities for four to six student teachers to train alongside UPCS faculty. This breeding ground tends to feed qualified young teachers into UPCS, as more than two-thirds of the faculty attended the Clark teacher-education program. Once on staff, teachers host rounds based on the medical model, so that senior teachers mentor younger ones, and all give each other feedback by using common planning time on Wednesday afternoons to review student work and their own lessons. When a teacher is out sick, a substitute isn't called; rather, another teacher takes over his or her class.

Since the partnership began, crime and transiency have gone down in the Main South neighborhood, and residential occupancy is up. Some families say they have moved in just so their children can attend University Park. Clark also provides additional benefits to its own faculty who live in the neighborhood, which Jack Foley describes as a "great incentive." First, any faculty member who buys a home in Main South receives $5,000 at the closing, a loan that is forgiven at the rate of $1,000 per year. In addition, for the first seven years they live there, faculty members receive an annual check of 12 percent of their salary, up to $4,000 per year. Finally, as with any local residents, if their children live in the neighborhood for five years and are admitted to Clark, they can attend for free. More than thirty faculty members have taken advantage of this program over the last eighteen years of its existence, and nineteen UPCS faculty members currently live in the neighborhood.

In addition, Clark welcomes UPCS students on its campus. The students are called "little Clarkies," carrying college IDs of their own. They can be found competing on the Clark athletic complex, studying at the university library, and attending campus events. Younger students are also welcome to enroll in mini-seminars with college professors from Clark—a favorite is the annual Shakespeare seminar for eighth graders. In grades eleven and twelve, students can even take courses at Clark, tuition free. To be eligible for these classes, students must have an honor roll average and get their teachers' approval; once they do, they receive college credit, and when they graduate from high school, they can enter college with advanced standing, saving them thousands of dollars in tuition. Two-thirds of students take at least one course before they graduate. The placements are so successful that Clark professors generally do not know which of their students are coming from UPCS and which are undergraduates.

IN THE EARLY days at UPCS, local parents—many of whom had never graduated from high school—were indifferent to the new, experimental school. To recruit the first class of students, the founding principal, Donna Rodrigues, talked up the school by going door to door. Rodrigues knew the neighborhood well as a long-time resident and Worcester public school teacher for twenty-eight years. She portrayed a safe school and challenging curriculum with educational opportunities for children, and the parents became intrigued. Parents were advised that their students would have to complete a minimum of two hours of homework every night, and students were required to attend a meeting informing them that they should not enroll if they were not ready to meet the challenge of a rigorous curriculum. "Having high expectations for the kids is really important," says former principal June Eressy. "Contrary to what many people think, these kids will rise to the occasion."

Soon a full class had enrolled at UPCS, and local families were enthusiastic about the new school. "Please tell me again that this is really true. It's too good for me. I've never been picked for anything good," said one father when Rodrigues told him his child would be attending University Park Campus School. In every subsequent year, there has been no need to recruit families; the demand is twice that of the available spots, which are allocated by lottery. Though admission is coveted, it is not begrudged any individuals who enter what local kids call "the smart school," as there are no selective criteria. Parents and kids describe being selected to enroll as winning the lotto jackpot.

Local parents are also a part of the collaboration, as the school tries to include them in the learning community. Struggling students receive weekly progress reports about homework completion, behavior, and upcoming assignments that each teacher fills out and parents sign and return. Family meetings are typically scheduled with all the student's core academic teachers. In addition, the lottery process includes all younger siblings of admitted students, so as to include entire families in the school community.

Since the process is randomized, the makeup of the school is truly representative of the demographics of the community: 75 percent are students of color, 88 percent receive free or reduced-price lunches, and 65 percent speak English as a second language. Many of the white students are recent immigrants from Eastern Europe who speak little or no English.

To date, the per pupil expenditure at UPCS—about $6,000 per year—is far lower than that at other Worcester public schools, and the lottery continues to be conducted at random. Nonetheless, the school has ranked first among urban schools serving low-income students on state English and math graduation exams and in the top quartile of all high schools in the state over the last four years. These tests—unlike other standardized tests, such as the SAT and ACT—actually reflect the ability of students to engage with material they have learned, as opposed to material that they may or may not have been exposed to, based on the economic and educational status of their families. The school's success has led to a high interest level by families in the community: approximately 75 percent of eligible students apply to UPCS. Unfortunately, the school can only accommodate about half its applicants.

Once enrolled, all the randomly selected students are expected to complete a full college-preparatory program. There are no placement tests or alternative tracks for different-level learners. "We don't have tracking because, to me, that is a sign that 'some of you are going to make it before the others,'" explains Rodrigues.

However, because there are no academic criteria within the admissions process, the vast majority of students enter at least two grade levels behind their age in reading and math. Ricci Hall, a former principal, describes the students who arrived at UPCS as "depleted." In a wonderful example of mission over admission, seventh graders entering UPCS attend the August Academy, a month-long summer program that introduces them to the academic rigor of UPCS and helps get them acclimated to its standards. The program consists of more than academics; it's also a chance for students to get to know their teachers, akin to a college orientation program for incoming freshmen. "We didn't have to be afraid of coming here," observed Jorge Ramirez, a UPCS senior.

Though they are aware of a wide achievement gap among students, the faculty are not daunted by it. Jim McDermott, a former UPCS English teacher, understood that the low proficiency levels were a problem of perception rather than a reflection of innate ability. Language is learned before the age of two, he points out, which is then reflected in the way we express ourselves and in our discourse and our dialect. Yet people tend to judge dialect and discourse as markers of intelligence, rather than indicators of social experience. McDermott's goal with UPCS students was to translate their individual abilities into traditional academic achievement. "The student who comes from the more affluent area speaks the school language more readily than does the person who comes from the more urban blighted area," he explains. "It's not that one is smarter than the other, but for years many teachers really treated one as being brighter than the other because he was more ready to understand the stories. So the gap grows and grows as the student gets older, and after a while the student looks at himself as being dumb."

Rather than trying to improve his students' prospects by emphasizing rote learning and drills to raise standardized-test scores, McDermott focused on their ability to engage in high-level independent thinking. "I wasn't trying to deal with my urban at-risk kids by giving them programs that Cambridge was giving to their urban at-risk kids," McDermott explains. "I was going to Phillips Exeter and Worcester Academy and figuring if it's good for those kids, then it's good for my kids. And what do they do at those schools? They have people sitting around tables talking about what they're writing, coming up with their own opinions. The thing is, having a thinking curriculum is not new; it's only new for at-risk urban poor kids."

This "thinking curriculum," bolstered by a focus on reading and writing, incorporates a lot of "low-stakes" writing—ungraded assignments that are exercises in creative freedom and encourage the students to draw on their own experiences. In their graded work, students are allowed to rewrite their essays as many times as necessary in order to score well and improve their reasoning and writing skills. As McDermott describes, it's "writing to learn," rather than "writing to show learning."

A decision not to teach to the test has consequences, of course. When the first round of UPCS students took the state proficiency exam, the Massachusetts Comprehensive Assessment System, or MCAS, the district sent a note to the school, warning that many of their performances on the multiple-choice portion were low and that they were in danger of failing. But McDermott took no action in response to the note because he was convinced the students would redeem themselves on the open-ended portion of the test. And he was right: all students in the first three classes passed the MCAS on the first try, and the vast majority scored at an advanced or proficient level. Overall, though only 40 percent of the students enter UPCS at an advanced or proficient level in English and math, 90 percent leave at those levels.

McDermott had an insight into the exam—after all, he was one of the educators enlisted to draft it. But his approach to open-ended writing is less about enhancing test performance than fostering his students' independence. "I think it's important that what it means to be an enlightened citizen is not just to take things as they are fed to us," he says. By encouraging its students to think for themselves, this community school creates a generation of problem solvers and innovators who can provide unique contributions to the community that raised them. "I don't want my kids learning history," McDermott opines. "Teach my kids to become young historians. This is what we say at University Park: don't teach science, teach your kids to be young scientists; don't teach literature, teach them to become young literary critics or writers."

DESPITE ITS SUCCESS, UPCS cannot ignore socioeconomic realities. Because class sizes are so small, the faculty is continually brought into the various personal and family crises of its student body. "The principal knows exactly what's going on," observes Kim Surrette, a UPCS student. She explains that when a student's grades begin to drop, the administrators take him or her aside to set up a "Game Plan" for improvement. In fact, the day before Kim was set to take an AP exam, her family was evicted from their apartment and became homeless. She recalls that throughout that day every teacher at UPCS approached her with offers to help. When Kim was planning to celebrate her birthday without a place to go home to, the principal called her into the office and handed her an envelope containing $150—all the teachers had pitched in to give her the gift. And in the cafeteria that day she was presented with a cupcake while everyone sang "Happy Birthday."

The faculty do their best to encourage their students, but ultimately the students must rise to the challenge. "I didn't pass out any failure warnings," recalls McDermott. "I handed out passing warnings. . . . If you do these certain things, I'm warning you, you'll pass. And some would. But it was on their shoulders, and they came around."

When students do succeed, the whole school acknowledges it; all college acceptances are posted on a bulletin board outside the guidance office, and when they are broadcast over the intercom during morning announcements, they receive a round of applause from students in classrooms.

ON THE WHOLE, students have risen to meet the high expectations. The seniors boast an attendance rate of 95 percent—and dropout rates of zero. In 2014, 100 percent of UPCS students were admitted to institutions of higher education: 89 percent to four-year colleges and 11 percent to two-year community colleges. These statistics are striking, even to the local residents. "Stereotypically, living in a neighborhood like this, you are not supposed to make it that far. You are not supposed to make it to college. You are destined to fail," says one alumnus, who went on to attend Brown University.

Meanwhile, Clark University has seen an incredible transformation of social consciousness on campus. The school has gained a sense of urban community, as well as having gained national visibility. It has begun attracting students who share this vision of service, who contribute to the community through ongoing involvement rather than, for example, dropping into a homeless shelter to volunteer for an hour or two.

This partnership has also provided possibilities for academic research from within the community, as opposed to a top-down approach. Jack

Foley, Clark's vice president for Government and Community Affairs and Campus Services, calls the neighborhood "a great laboratory" that currently attracts faculty who want to work in the neighborhood, from sociology and psychology professors to researchers collecting mental health data and analyzing the market forces of rehabilitating an urban area.

As a result, Clark has become nationally known as a leader in university-community partnerships. The press coverage that has resulted from the partnership has benefited the university's public relations and alumni-giving efforts, as well as outside fund-raising drives. University Park's reputation for successful student achievement has grown as well, so that now the school, along with Clark University and the nonprofit Jobs for the Future, cosponsors a professional development institute for school teams from early-college high schools across the country. "It helps us to know the world is watching," says Foley.

THE SUCCESS OF UPCS has led to another partnership in Worcester, a "fascinating story," as Jack Foley describes it. Claremont Academy was an underperforming school in the same neighborhood as UPCS, just blocks away from Clark on the other side of campus. Yet while UPCS thrived, Claremont was struggling to achieve academic success and being threatened with state sanctions if it failed to improve.

Clark realized that reviving this school was important toward rebuilding the neighborhood, Tom Del Prete explains, adding, "We had this outstanding model in UPCS." However, the start-up conditions were very different: Claremont was a pre-existing school, whereas Clark had started as a partner with UPCS from its inception.

In fact, when the Worcester school committee intervened under state pressure and split off grades seven through twelve from the K–12 school, Clark's offer to help with the restructure of Claremont didn't get a lot of traction. "The culture wasn't ready to embrace the partnership," Del Prete recalls.

In 2012, however, the principal of Claremont left the school, and the superintendent saw an opportunity to take it in a new direction. Ricci

Hall, then the principal of UPCS, took leadership of Claremont, and Clark committed to being a full partner in the new venture. Four UPCS senior teachers and the guidance counselor followed Hall to Claremont. Those openings in the UPCS staff were filled by Clark alumni who had completed their teaching year in the master's program.

Despite this commitment from UPCS and Clark, the partnership with Claremont was not immediately embraced. In fact, there was a heated conflict with the teachers' union, and half the Claremont teachers left the school rather than join in the new vision. Those in the partnership questioned how much restaffing was needed, believing there should be a critical mass of new talent but hoping to keep enough former teachers to help the transition. After a tremendous fight with the union, the school was almost entirely restaffed over the summer, and Clark sponsored a week of professional development for new and returning teachers.

Many students also felt loyal to Claremont as it had been, and it became clear that Claremont needed to build community support in order to succeed. A local city councilwoman and a UPCS parent gathered other local leaders, including a Latino community organizer and a church minister, to get more people invested in the venture. They created an advisory board and held a meeting that included mental health professionals, ministers, Clark faculty, and members of the local Boys and Girls Club. Meanwhile, Principal Ricci Hall went door to door to discuss Claremont's new offerings with parents and distribute literature in English, Spanish, and Vietnamese. "Culture change is not simple," Del Prete observes, but they soon began "seeing signs of good things happening" as local families began to express interest in Claremont.

Unlike UPCS, Claremont is a neighborhood school with open admission to all local students, rather than through a lottery. There is some overlap with the area covered by UPCS, and 75 percent of those students enter that lottery in addition to applying to Claremont. Students also have the option of attending the larger area high school, which some choose at least in part for its athletic offerings, which the smaller schools lack. As for Claremont, Del Prete says, "We're determined that it is going to be parallel to UPCS."

With that in mind, Del Prete identifies four main aspects of the UPCS–Clark partnership that Claremont aspires to model. ("'Replication' is a word we avoid," he cautions, pointing out that every joint venture is different.) The first and most basic goal is simply to make the university part of the curriculum for the high school students. The intention is to dissolve the boundary between the school and the campus and expose the students to college life in a strategic way, thus creating a relative seamlessness between high school and college rather than enforcing the feeling that Claremont graduates have to "jump the walls" to go to college. In a community where many families do not consider college a viable option, the partnership wants to build that aspiration.

The second aspect of UPCS that Claremont seeks to model is its "powerful learning" agenda. The question, Del Prete explains, is how to create a culture of independent learning and to create a community "around the idea that you can all go to college and are outstanding young people." Claremont hopes to create a high level of student engagement and give robust support to those who are struggling to learn—as well as incorporating some "controlled failure." The students are taught self-reliance and how to negotiate new spaces so that they are prepared to succeed in college.

After all, one of the big lessons drawn from the last five years at UPCS, Del Prete notes, was "getting better at shifting the responsibility for learning to the kids." The students must learn to be proactive about getting help, whether that means joining a study group or reaching out to a faculty member or taking other steps. To that end, Claremont provides a seminar to seniors, taught by Clark graduate students and supervised by Clark faculty, to assist not only with college applications but also college preparation. These seminars are a far cry from the expensive college-prep classes where students learn and plan in a silo and an atmosphere of competition is fostered. "Finally, we're united," Del Prete exults. "We've created this neighborhood-based approach, one we've envisioned, with neighborhood partners. Everyone benefits." Even Clark faculty outside of the education field have volunteered to help in these college-prep classes, and some professors teach mini-courses at Claremont or UPCS. Another idea that has been floated is a class in conjunction with the Clark theater department, to give high school students a new way of thinking and a way to express themselves outside of the traditional curriculum.

The third aspect of UPCS that Claremont hopes to model is its collaborative approach to teaching. Clark graduate students assist at Claremont, and the school encourages teachers to work in teams and learn from each other's classes. How teachers learn together will have a big impact on students' learning, Del Prete says. The goal is to build a professional culture devoted to working with struggling students.

Finally, Claremont aspires to model the high level of community involvement in UPCS. As noted, it has an advisory board composed of local citizens, as does UPCS. One of the programs proposed and enacted by the board was an internship program based in the community. Local citizens identify opportunities for students, and seniors from both schools work in these varied placements. Some observe operations at a bank while others visit classrooms or local businesses for three hours on Friday mornings. The teachers use that time to meet for curriculum-planning purposes.

A big question for Clark in working with Claremont faculty was how to focus all the teachers on the new mission for the school, provide professional development, and structure their leadership. It settled on a distributive-leadership model, identifying one or two leaders for every two grades. Clark also supports a literacy position there to provide funding and instruction.

At the end of the day, Claremont needs the support of all interested parties to be successful. "How do you help kids who want to engage in demanding activity," Del Prete queries, "and also begin to appreciate themselves as learners, future thinkers, and problem solvers?" He concedes that these are "challenging questions" but concludes, "It's great to work in partnership to answer them."

—m—

DESPITE THE INCREDIBLE results it has achieved within its small, supportive learning community, UPCS has struggled to promote its students' success beyond its own campus. Many of the first-generation college attenders have gotten lost in larger schools and failed to complete their degrees. For example, everyone who attended the University of Massachusetts at Amherst dropped out before graduation, as did all the first year's admits to Clark. Jack Foley admits, "We missed the first year, and we're trying to catch up."

In the years since then, there has been an increased focus on college readiness and the transition to college, according to former principal Ricci Hall. She and others realized that their students were having problems managing their time, advocating for themselves, and finding necessary resources. In addition to selecting students to take classes for credit at Clark, the administrators instituted a requirement a few years later that all UPCS students must at least audit a college course before graduation. This added exposure to college-level work appears to agree with the high schoolers. Foley notes that the UPCS students can now keep up with the college courses, and in fact, some have done "too well," in his opinion—"better than the college students!"

Initially, the UPCS teachers did so much to engage the students and make the material come alive that the students were unprepared for the hands-off approach to teaching at many colleges. As Hall observes, in college much of the learning occurs outside the classroom, when students study on their own, which is the polar opposite of the interactive classes at UPCS. It was that "inquiry-based approach" that UPCS developed—promoting student engagement and critical, analytical thinking—that actually made it difficult for UPCS students to direct their own studies in college.

Daniel St. Louis, the current principal of UPCS and a former teacher there, addressed this issue by presenting a PowerPoint lecture to the students in one anatomy class and presenting the same material in a more interactive format the next. He then asked the students which one worked best for them. Though most preferred the interactive form, some were content to take in the material in a lecture-based form. Regardless of the students' preference, St. Louis wanted to help the students "understand themselves as thinkers," he explains, rather than wait for the professors to identify how students learned best and how to accommodate their learning styles.

St. Louis recalls that, at the conclusion of his demonstration of different teaching styles, one of his students commented in surprise, "It's like you planned this!" He was supremely complimented but also disturbed. After all the effort that the UPCS teachers had put into developing their pedagogy, the students were unaware of how the lessons had been constructed to promote their learning.

The faculty realized that they had to help their students understand the structural framework that had been supporting them throughout middle school and high school, so that the students could re-create this structure for themselves after graduation. It was a matter of "uncovering the scaffolding," Ricci Hall explains. The teachers needed to help students develop the skills necessary to break down challenging material on their own.

As it turned out, the students were so used to a high level of support that they were floundering without it. As Hall puts it, they were in a "well-lit room" in high school, but then the light went off when they moved on to college, and the students were left in the dark. The challenge for the faculty was to create a dimmer switch, Hall says, so that they could slowly shift responsibility for deconstructing the material to the students. Although most of the students entering UPCS in grades seven and eight were coming in below grade level and needed intensive academic support, Hall instructed his faculty to carefully dial back the level of support they provided to students as the grade level increased.

Another major problem for UPCS graduates in college is adjusting to campus life. Sending students who grew up in a triple-decker with ten siblings and two parents, many living on disability income, to places like Middlebury and Tufts was "like putting them on the moon," Hall explains. UPCS now employs a full-time alumni support coordinator, and the guidance counselor, teachers, and principal also reach out to seniors who plan to go away to school, to discuss the impending culture shock.

In addition to providing basic services like helping students fill out financial aid forms and decipher syllabi, the alumni coordinator, along with the rest of the staff, discusses students' concerns about fitting in. Students typically raise questions about financial constraints, like what to do when all their friends are going out for beers and pizza, and they don't have any money.

It became clear that, rather than coming into college with a sense of entitlement, as paying customers demanding a service, the UPCS students were often insecure about whether they belonged and whether they were worthy of their spot in the class. The faculty encouraged them to realize that they did possess critical-thinking skills at a college level. When pressed, students admitted feeling confident in their writing skills, as well as in speaking and presenting, given all the participation required of them at UPCS. As Hall notes, they are "dynamite, dedicated, personable people" who can be campus leaders, if only they are given the opportunity and can be convinced of their own worth. Hall continually reminds graduates that not only do they possess the ability to succeed in college, but they bring a valuable perspective to the campus that other students benefit from. "You are getting a lot from the school," Hall tells them, "but you are also an asset."

In recognition of the value UPCS students bring, Clark has also taken steps to support them. Those who matriculate to Clark now attend a pre-orientation summer session, and all have the same faculty advisor in the Hiatt Center for Urban Education. The hope is that UPCS alumni will support one another, both socially and academically. Hall describes the "cohorts of supportive alumni" he wants to gather; these cohorts would connect with incoming students to provide mentorship and guidance. The program is not yet as robust as he would like, but UPCS continues to work toward this goal, which fits more broadly with the school's mission. As Hall puts it, "We are a community, and we can always achieve more together."

CHAPTER FIVE

No Longer Lonely at the Top: The Posse Foundation

DESPITE THE GAINS made by the students at University Park Campus School in Worcester, their academic success often came to a halt outside the high school hallways. This was not as a result of their supposedly lower intellect or from a lack of dedication. Many students struggle at the higher echelons of education for very different reasons: because they have trouble advocating for themselves or finding necessary resources, because they have never learned the principles of time management, or simply because they suffer from insecurity as to whether or not they "belong." As it turns out, for certain students, such as children of parents who did not go to college or in some cases didn't even go to high school, gaining admission to college is only the beginning of the battle; adjusting to college life proves in some cases to be even harder than getting in. This is where democratic merit can truly shine: when students work together to solve problems and make advances, rather than scratch their lonely way to the top, they can create a supportive learning environment, one I find wonderfully embodied by The Posse Foundation.

In the fall of 1989, a twenty-three-year-old Brandeis University graduate named Debbie Bial was running a New York City youth leadership program when she met a young black man from East Harlem who had recently walked away from what she describes as "a major scholarship at a major university." The student was known to be academically gifted; his friends had nicknamed him "Stein" for "Einstein." When Bial asked him why he had dropped out, he responded, "I could have done it if I had had my posse with me."

From this remark came the idea for The Posse Foundation, which each year helps urban public high school students to win full, four-year merit scholarships from "top-ranked" colleges. Currently in its twenty-fifth year, the foundation recruits students from Atlanta, Boston, Chicago, Houston, Los Angeles, Miami, New Orleans, New York, and Washington, DC; it has fifty-one partner universities to date. Since its start in 1989, when the foundation recruited five New York City students to attend Vanderbilt University in Nashville, Tennessee, more than 5,500 students have received over $680 million in scholarships.

The foundation's principal missions are, one, to identify promising urban public high school students who lack the traditional testocratic indicators of success, such as high SAT scores, and two, to send these students on to college in groups of ten, which they call "posses." Although the foundation does not take race into account in its selection process, most of its scholars are students of color, thanks to the racial and ethnic make-up of the city high schools from which the foundation recruits. Because these students often find themselves overwhelmed by the cultural and academic differences between their high schools and the elite, majority-white colleges they enter as freshmen, the posses serve as critical peer-support networks.

We all have times in our life when we are feeling lonely, when the situation we are in feels overwhelming. I remember working for the NAACP Legal Defense and Educational Fund (LDF) after I left my position at the Justice Department as special assistant to Assistant Attorney General for Civil Rights Drew S. Days III. My LDF team was sent to Arkansas to try a case. There were three of us: myself (a black woman), a white woman, and a black paralegal. There were no restaurants available in the part of Arkansas we were in after five o'clock, so we'd have to cross the river to Mississippi to eat. I think we went maybe twice to this

Mississippi restaurant, and the first time we could hear the people in the kitchen saying, "They say they're from New York."

My coworkers at the LDF were my posse, and they helped me cope with the feeling of being a stranger in a strange land; we helped each other in this tense situation. Posse Foundation alumni have recounted facing similar cultural barriers when they started college. Danielle Berry, a Posse scholar at the University of Wisconsin at Madison, says her first weekend visiting campus was "the worst weekend of my life. I didn't see another African American the whole time I was [there]. I actually went into a store . . . and asked the clerk where all the black people were. I couldn't believe what I'd gotten myself into." But when Berry was put on academic probation, two other Posse students pushed her to get on top of her studies. "Jai and Dominique and I were like a Super Posse," she told the alumni magazine On Wisconsin. "Especially Jai; I think of her like a big sister. They were very honest with me, even when I didn't want to hear it." Thanks to this support, Berry says, "I was more comfortable. I was meeting other people, being myself," and doing better academically. By the summer of her junior year, Berry was confident and upbeat enough to assert that everything was "falling into place for me. I feel like I know my purpose. And I feel like I can help other people." Danielle not only graduated from Wisconsin but went on to get her master of science degree in journalism from Roosevelt University.

David Perez Jr., a Posse scholar and class of 1997 Vanderbilt University alumnus, completed his PhD in education at Pennsylvania State University in 2010, but he was out of his element when he first began school. A Puerto Rican kid who grew up in pre-gentrified Williamsburg, Brooklyn, David had joined a gang when he was in his mid-teens to gain status in his neighborhood, and he was cutting school and failing all of his classes. In and out of different high schools, David eventually fell two full academic years behind and finally finished his studies at an alternative high school for students with chronic problems. He worked hard there, doubling up on his courses and excelling academically. A teacher took an interest in David and nominated him for a Posse Foundation scholarship, back when the program was still fairly new. David was stunned when he received the news that he had been selected to matriculate at Vanderbilt University with a full scholarship. He had never heard of the university before.

David did not have a smooth transition to college life. "It wasn't the first time I was away from home, but it was the first time I was on my own," he says of his experience. "My mom was able to scratch pennies together to get me a plane ticket, and I went to Nashville with a word processor, which was a pretty big deal."

David felt like a complete outsider when he first arrived at Vanderbilt. He looked at the students' cars—Mercedes, Saabs, and Porsches—and calculated that many students drove automobiles with price tags greater than his mother's annual salary. Nothing about him—from his limited wardrobe to the way his noisy, cheap word processor stuck out amid his roommates' state-of-the-art computers—blended in. Having the campus police stop him and question his student status one night seemed to confirm to David that he didn't belong. He didn't even bother to unpack his clothes for the first six weeks of school and called his mother every day because he was so homesick.

By the middle of the first semester, David was convinced that the best thing for him to do was to drop out of Vanderbilt and go back home. He was getting up the courage to break the news to his mother when Erica Spatz, one of the members of his posse, happened to stop by his room one day. "She saw that my bag was not unpacked, and she was like, 'Let's go to the store and get some hangers.' We began to put my clothes on hangers, and that moment was very symbolic of the fact that I was then going to stay."

Though he resolved to stick it out at Vanderbilt, David struggled in his classes. As a first-generation college student from an alternative public high school, he hadn't cultivated the study skills or familiarity with academic language, such as how to decode a syllabus, which he needed to hit the ground running in college. Like some graduates from University Park Campus School, he also hadn't yet mastered how to organize his time. By the end of the first semester, David had the lowest GPA in his posse: a near-failing 1.3. The dean placed him on academic probation, and David realized that he would have to start asking for help if he was going to succeed academically.

With the support of his posse, professors, and various mentors, David was able to turn things around. He got off academic probation in only one semester, bringing his GPA up to a 2.5. "A lot of it was learning through the process of being with others," he explains. "I would watch people in my posse and ask how do they know what to read for class? Why are they working on that paper now if it's not due? How do you put together a calendar?" David enrolled in study-skills classes at Vanderbilt's learning center, which helped him with time management, critical reading skills, and writing. "There were also a lot of faculty who were really invested in The Posse Foundation, so when I was placed on academic probation, I met with a caring faculty member who really helped me," he says.

Of all the people who helped him, David singles out his mentor, Shirley Collado, an older and more experienced Posse student at Vanderbilt. The daughter of Dominican immigrants, Shirley was a member of the very first group of Posse scholars to enroll in college, in 1989. Like David, Shirley grew up in Brooklyn and was the first in her family to attend college. Her father drove a New York City taxicab and her mother worked at a factory.

Shirley understood the culture shock that David was experiencing. Her father, a traditional Dominican man, was initially against Shirley leaving home to enroll in college in Tennessee. She says her parents didn't have a sense of the difference between Vanderbilt or a local community college and couldn't understand why she needed to go so far from home to attend school. Shirley's grandmother was able to persuade her father to let Shirley go under one condition: Shirley had to agree to speak to her father every night at 8 p.m., when he would call her from a pay phone. He wanted to keep the family rules, Shirley explains, to let her know that going away was a privilege, and she agreed to abide by them. "It was an enormous sacrifice on his part," she says. "I felt like this was the least I could do." They spoke every day throughout her first few years of school, strengthening her ties to her community and providing constant support from back home. At first Shirley thought those nightly phone calls were for her father's sake, but she soon found out they were far more beneficial for her. Conversing with her father gave him an opportunity to reinforce his confidence in her, even as the experiences she was having were a lot to take. Though her father had not gone to college, he was able to be an effective mentor for Shirley and gave her the skills to mentor David in turn.

Because Shirley was a few years ahead of David, she was able to help him adapt to the academic rituals and demands of Vanderbilt University. Shirley would invite David to join her during her study time at the library. She got out her datebook and showed him how to manage a schedule. She helped him get a job at the campus bookstore so he could get a discount on textbooks and wouldn't have to rely as much on his mother for funds. "There was a point where I kind of gave up on myself, but I think those interactions enhanced my self-efficacy and made me realize that I could take certain steps to get through Vanderbilt," David says.

With the help of his mentors and peers, David eventually adjusted to life at Vanderbilt. He took advantage of a study-abroad opportunity and went to London for a semester. He became a resident advisor in a dormitory, made dean's list, and started contemplating graduate school.

As David began to flourish at Vanderbilt, he started to look for ways to give back. "I made it a point to extend myself in any way possible to a new Posse student, because I remembered how hard it was for me," he says. When he returned for his sophomore year, he quickly reached out to the new students, befriending one student in particular—another Puerto Rican boy from New York—who also happened to share his last name. "He was encountering a lot of the same challenges: feeling isolated, kind of struggling academically. I spent time with him, talking to him about how things were going. I got a sense of how he was doing things so that I could figure out how to help him," David says of his friend.

The following year, when he was a junior, David made it a point to look after Carlos, a Dominican boy from New York City who was still suffering the raw wounds of his brother's murder from several years before. Whenever something bad happened at school—if Carlos broke up with a girlfriend or got cut from the baseball team—he would post negative quotes or phrases on a bulletin board outside his dorm room. Remembering how bleak things had seemed to him when he first matriculated at Vanderbilt, David wanted to help raise Carlos's spirits. So, every night, he would replace one of Carlos's pessimistic slogans with something positive. "It became a battle, and we talked about it," David says of the exchange. "I told him, 'I know I'm not in your position, but you're going to get through this.' Our relationship was stronger because of these fights. We still stay connected."

Shirley also felt compelled to share her success with others who came through the program after her. She went on to get her PhD at Duke, although without her posse, she says, "it was one of the hardest things I've ever done." When the atmosphere of collaborative learning that Shirley had embraced—and mirrored for others—was replaced by one of individual achievement she struggled. But she was motivated to set an example of academic success for other Posse scholars. "I wanted my story to help colleges and universities believe in people like me," she explains.

TO FORM ITS POSSES, the foundation relies on nominations from school guidance counselors and other community partners to gather an initial group of students who show promise beyond what their performances on conventional measures of testable merit might indicate. Nominated students receive a letter that says, "Congratulations. You have been nominated by someone in your community for a $100,000 scholarship because you are outstanding."

So begins a three-and-a-half-month process, with multiple rounds, throughout which the selection committee highlights students' strengths and their potential to enrich the campuses of the colleges that seek to recruit them. Since the selection is both need-blind and race-blind, there is no emphasis on increasing numbers of different groups on campus but rather on selecting the next generation of leaders from an often-overlooked pool of students from disadvantaged neighborhoods. As a result, there is no accompanying stigma to becoming a Posse scholar and no implication that schools are lowering their standards by including the Posse scholars.

One donor who gives financial support to the Posse program at his alma mater said he does so because it's not a traditional affirmative action program. "It isn't about numbers but about recruiting high-quality students," he said. "It's about identifying leadership potential. Posse provides a group of kids who know how to deal with the diversity issue. They aren't just going to go to class and take up space. They're leaders. They're involved. They're the kind of students you really want to have on campus."

One of the most innovative features of The Posse Foundation is its selection process. During the initial screening, foundation staff members do not consider those pervasive standards of competitive merit seen on traditional college applications such as test scores, grades, and extracurricular activities. Rather they use what they call the Dynamic Assessment Process (DAP), which measures collaborative merit instead. Staff members give nominated students several group assignments ("interactive workshops") and evaluate them on leadership ability, the ability to get along with people from different cultural backgrounds, the quality of thinking, and their desire to succeed—all traits the foundation has identified as predictors of academic success in college.

The foundation invites back approximately 60 percent of this initial group for follow-up interviews and, together with college admissions officers, assembles "posses" of roughly ten students per institution. The college gives each Posse member a four-year, full-tuition merit scholarship.

Nominees tend to find value in the foundation's selection process in and of itself. "I remember the first round being the best interview that I have ever had," says Daniel Acheampong, a Posse scholar at Brandeis from Crown Heights, Brooklyn. "It wasn't just the interview. You go there and see hundreds of kids. It was about being creative. . . . I was like, 'This is exciting. I'm going to have fun here.'" Other Posse scholars agree. "I think it felt less like an interview and more of a positive experience where you could see how ideas are formed and learn how to communicate with different people you had never met before," says Mosi London, a Posse scholar who graduated from Lafayette College. Since this process often represents the students' first experiences interviewing, many nominees find that process useful as well. "I plan to go to medical school, and in any career you need to do some kind of interviewing, so the more experience I get in that, the better," says Angel Garcia, a Posse scholar at Brandeis.

Rather than viewing "merit" as a fixed and measurable quality that students demonstrate to gain entrance, The Posse Foundation continues to cultivate students' potential for innovation and leadership after they are selected to receive the scholarship. Before they even set foot on a college campus, Posse scholars embark on an eight-month weekly training program to prepare them for higher education. Each week, posses gather to focus on four areas: (1) team building and group support, (2) cross-cultural communication, (3) leadership, and (4) academic excellence. The training focuses equally on preparing students academically and preparing them for personal challenges, such as time and money management and interacting with a majority-white student body that is considerably better off than those in their high schools. A range of topics are discussed, including race, diversity, sexual orientation, and class, which helps to prepare students for conversations on these topics once they arrive on campus. Students are encouraged to cultivate self-awareness, which helps them set and achieve goals, and to prepare for the challenges they might face in college. At the end of the eight months, Posse members attend a weekend retreat outside the city.

Daniel Acheampong recalls that the pre-college training program "felt a little forced in the beginning," but he conceded that "it was really good to get to know each other." Looking back, he reflects, "I think they were training us to be supportive of each other. They wanted us to see that there was a difference between going to campus as a 'posse' and just being a collection of students who happen to have a scholarship." Right from the beginning, Posse scholars are encouraged to view each other as collaborators and to understand that they are stronger as a unit than as an assortment of individuals.

Daniel and his posse enrolled at Brandeis after completing the pre-college training program. As part of the scholarship requirements, the group continued to meet weekly and members were assigned to work with on-campus mentor Ashley Rondini, a PhD student in philosophy and sociology. In addition to the group meetings, Daniel and Ashley met individually twice a month for Daniel's first two years of college. "She was willing to give up almost anything for us as a posse," Daniel recalls. "She went through so much herself, but she was always there. She would find a way to help you if you needed it and did a really good job of bringing us all together and making us realize that we're not friends—we're family."

Daniel's Posse family came out in full force when he decided to run for student body treasurer in his sophomore year. Not only did his posse help him with campaign materials like posters, fliers, and e-mails, but they also provided the support he needed to take the emotional risk of running for a campus office. "Posse had a lot to do with that," he says of his courage to run. "Everyone on campus knows what Posse is, and the support system we have is really strong."

In addition to assigning an on-campus mentor (usually a graduate student or a member of the faculty or college staff), universities designate a liaison to stay in regular contact with the foundation, and four times a year, a foundation member visits the college. Additionally, every spring the foundation sponsors a PossePlus retreat, in which Posse members and members of the larger student body meet to discuss a campus issue chosen by Posse members. Recently, the foundation initiated a career program, which helps Posse students secure internships at organizations in the United States and abroad (supplying a stipend for students doing unpaid internships) and helps Posse alumni to connect with potential employers. The career program maintains an active alumni network (there are currently more than 1,500 Posse alumni and more than 1,600 Posse scholars on campuses), provides job-search training (individually or in group workshops), and facilitates a mentoring relationship between Posse grads and current Posse students.

Yvonne Perez, another Posse scholar at Brandeis, explains the culture of the Posse program at the university: "Posse at Brandeis is very well known for being made up of leaders. Behind every aspect of student life, you see a Posse scholar. We realize that you can't keep yourself behind your books all the time. I saw other Posse scholars going out of their way to get involved in campus and still excelling academically. Having that great model to follow, I found what interests me on campus and went about doing it." Yvonne is a co-coordinator of a Hispanic group called AHORA (Hispanic and Latino/a Student Association) and has organized Hispanic Heritage Month events on campus. Along with several members of her posse, Yvonne also helped found a Brandeis chapter of the Society for the Advancement of Chicanos and Native Americans in Science.

FOLLOWING GRADUATION, many Posse scholars have demonstrated a commitment to public service. Both David and Shirley went on to pursue careers as educators and focused on expanding opportunities for underserved students, for which they credit their experience in The Posse Foundation's career program. "There's no question that I would not be where I am today but for or because of Posse," David says. "It has pretty much dictated the career that I wanted to pursue."

After graduating from Vanderbilt, David took a position in a residential treatment center doing conflict resolution and family therapy for inner-city youth, a job he learned about from one of his peers in his posse. He then returned to Vanderbilt for his master's degree in education and became a mentor to Vanderbilt Posse 10. "I felt that serving in that position was my calling," David says. "I just knew that this was something that I wanted to do forever."

David has since worked in diversity and youth development programs at Syracuse and New York universities, ultimately attaining his PhD in higher education at Pennsylvania State University with a focus on high-achieving Latino male college students. "Rather than focusing on those in crisis, I want to interview the ones who get through and identify those factors that contribute to their success to figure out how to help the ones who don't make it," David explains. His goal is to influence education policy and expand college access for underserved students in order to provide others with the same opportunities that Posse gave to him.

Shirley was the first Posse student to earn a doctorate (hers was in clinical psychology). After doing community mental health work, she went back to work with The Posse Foundation, serving as its executive vice president for six years. She later worked in the administration of Middlebury and Lafayette colleges. In 2010, she returned to Middlebury as vice president for student affairs and dean of the college. In January 2015, she will serve as executive vice chancellor for strategic initiatives and executive vice provost at Rutgers University–Newark. Shirley describes herself as a "quiet revolutionary," someone working within the system of selective, predominantly white institutions to bring about change and inclusiveness.

To that end, Shirley believes that her experience as a Posse scholar gives her an insider's view of the program and insights into the needs of Posse scholars. As part of the first cohort of Posse scholars, Shirley initially thought her experience of going to a selective college was unique. But she soon realized that hers was a typical story of coming to Posse as a first-generation college attendee from an immigrant family. "There were a lot of other versions of that story," she observes.

At Middlebury, Shirley says, the Posse program has been "so much more than a way to get a critical mass" of students of color. Posse's presence on campus is a "true partnership," she says, and not just as a pipeline for recruiting low-income students or a means of outsourcing admissions. In the fall of 2012, Middlebury added a cohort from Chicago to its original group from New York City because the program had found such success. And in 2014, the college added a Posse STEM (science, technology, engineering, and mathematics) cohort from Los Angeles, which will matriculate in the fall of 2015. That will bring to Middlebury three posses—a total of 120 scholars by 2018. "The Posse program has allowed us as an institution to ask the hard questions," she says of the partnership. "How do we act and think about diversity and community and inclusion?"

Ultimately, Shirley sees the Posse program as a way to think about admissions in a more holistic way. The real question, she says, is how to make sure students from all backgrounds fully participate in and get the full benefit of their education, whether they are coming from Posse on a scholarship or from Connecticut and paying a full ride. Shirley aspires to "take what we know works with Posse and bring it to the rest of the institution." Mentoring works, she observes, and cohorts work.

Posse's approach, says Shirley, is having a ripple effect on the rest of the school. For example, the first-year orientation program went through a major overhaul. Students are now broken into cohorts and take trips as a part of orientation, which can consist of outdoor excursions or cultural, political, or agricultural outings. Over the course of three days, the students are in dialogue with one another, and the groups are engineered to be racially and ethnically diverse as well as mixed in terms of life experience. Also included in orientation is an intensive workshop around identity called "Middlebury Uncensored," which encourages the students to challenge their assumptions about others and have difficult discussions that touch on race, sexual orientation, and financial situations, as well as personal fears and anxieties. Orientation is facilitated by peer leaders and is mandatory for all first-year students, including varsity athletes.

"There is no way of measuring or starting to imagine the impact of Posse on the faculty," Shirley adds, noting that faculty describe their experiences with the program as transformational. "Posse has changed mentors in a way that Posse never imagined and mentors never imagined."

Miguel Fernandez, a Spanish professor and former Posse mentor agrees, calling his involvement in Posse "one of the most rewarding experiences I've had as an educator." He describes his Posse scholars as a "remarkable, incredible group." At weekly meetings, they talked about different issues the students were facing, such as social life, roommate problems, and racist comments made in class. "Why do these white people want to drink all night and no one is interested in dancing?" he recalls his students asking. In the group, the Posse scholars were often able to address one another's concerns, teaching Fernandez how to handle various issues that affected many of his students. "The social piece is very, very important," he says, "and can be as challenging as the academics, if not more so."

Fernandez observes that general admissions to the school have begun to take a more holistic view of students, as well, considering additional information beyond grades, test scores, and activities. Yet he bemoans Middlebury's continued lack of diversity among its faculty. "Middlebury has failed at that," he observes, noting that there are few role models for students of color.

Nonetheless, the school has managed to find mentors who have successfully led and learned from their posses. Roger Sandwick, for example, was not the usual suspect to mentor a diverse group of young urban students. A white male chemistry professor in his late fifties, he describes himself as a "country hick" who gets nervous about taking the subway. He says he didn't know what to expect when he agreed to serve as a Posse mentor. "When I took it on, I hardly knew what Posse was," he recalls.

That summer, Sandwick attended a weekend retreat on campus to get to know the students. He also attended a training session, whereupon he was told, "Don't be their parent; be their mentor." But that lesson never stuck. "I was bad at that—I was their parent. I loved them to death," he confesses. Sandwick admits having had a hard time being objective: if his students were upset, he was upset; if a professor slighted them, he felt slighted and resentful.

Meanwhile, many members of his posse struggled upon their arrival on a campus full of rich kids, with few students of color and fewer students from urban environments. Middlebury is in "the middle of nowhere," Sandwick admits, noting that the closest big town, the small city of Burlington, is an hour away. For his students, it was as big a culture shock as anything, he explains. More than one of his students was surprised to learn that yellow dandelions grew from the fuzzy white weeds they saw on the ground.

Yet Sandwick was bowled over by the qualities his posse brought to campus, in addition to their diverse viewpoints as urban public school kids in a largely suburban prep school student population. "Oh my God, you guys are so much smarter than me," he recalls thinking, amazed at how articulate they were.

In the end, Sandwick concludes, "they taught me more than I taught them." Specifically, he was reminded about the social pressures that students faced, particularly in dating and dorm life, and he learned to be more compassionate to students. "The whole dating scene was something I didn't know about," he confesses. But working with the students gave him the opportunity to see students as individuals. "I try to listen more to the students, to the internal struggles they have," Sandwick says. Moreover, his posse brought him out of his shell a little. He concedes that he is by nature reserved and bashful, and that his students taught him to take chances, reassuring him that he had nothing to lose. At the Posse retreat, they'd cheer him on to speak publicly and participate in group activities.

IN GENERAL, SANDWICK admits that his students didn't excel academically, although all of them ultimately graduated. He believes the problem is with the pedagogy and not with the Posse scholars. "Grading in college is similar to grading in prep school: students are told by their professors, 'Here is the information, now repeat it back; here is my view, now regurgitate it.'" As a chemist, Sandwick thinks that he and his colleagues are some of the worst perpetuators of this "spit it back" approach. But that's not how it should be, he says. "I don't think that's what intelligence is all about."

Sandwick shares the view of the two educators I will feature in the next chapter. Part of what his posse taught him was to credit different learning styles and to give students different kinds of assignments. "If you just do it one way, a certain population of students will rise to the top," says Sandwick. In the sciences, he admits, they often employ the "regurgitation method," where there is only one right answer, much like the SAT. "We have to do things better," he concludes. "The regurgitation method doesn't get you the best students, like my posse."

This method certainly suited the typical Middlebury student, however. "The prep school students are trained to take an SAT, and they're ready to come on campus and excel in the type of education that we champion," Sandwick says. Yet this method of teaching caused several Posse scholars to fall short of their academic goals. Some came to school wanting to be pre-med, Sandwick recounts, but they soon dropped that course of study and switched majors, though "not because they weren't smart or going to be good doctors or scientists." In fact, one of Sandwick's students was an especially smart young woman who had won prestigious fellowships and was a leader among her peers. "Everyone knew her on campus," Sandwick recalls, and she knew where all the resources were, so she'd direct other members of her posse to where they needed to go. But she couldn't handle the math in her introductory chemistry course, so she ultimately majored in psychology. She now plans to go to graduate school in clinical psychology, but, says Sandwick with a sigh, "I worry about that GRE score for her."

In the present-day testocracy, Sandwick's fears for his student's future may well come to pass. Meanwhile, however, Posse's influence has been expanding among undergraduate institutions. New schools are added as partners every year, allowing the foundation to expand to more cities: by 2020, the foundation expects to have seven thousand alumni. The program comes with a hefty price tag: even at a state school like the University of Wisconsin at Madison, the cost of four years of full tuition for a posse of ten out-of-state scholars is nearly $1 million. Yet the foundation's success at attracting college and university partners despite the cost is largely attributable to its skill at matching an often overlooked supply of talented high school students (most but not all of color) with a growing demand among majority-white colleges for ways to diversify their campuses without resorting to race-based affirmative action programs, which are increasingly maligned by the public and disfavored by the courts.

The Posse Foundation does this largely by redefining merit as something other than cumulative GPA and SAT and AP scores, and focusing instead on characteristics such as leadership, the ability to collaborate with and learn from others, and drive. This is an important factor in the effort to shift the idea of merit from being individualistic and competitive to being pluralistic and supportive. Of course, as I've noted repeatedly, universities have long prized such traits as predictive of student success, and since the advent of the SAT and other standardized tests in the 1940s, they have relied heavily on such quantifiable, comparable measures of ability for their objectivity and to place less significance on an applicant's "noncognitive" skills, which are seen as immeasurable and elusive. To assess them is an inherently subjective process, making it difficult to compare candidates across localities or institutions. By emphasizing traits like leadership and collaboration, Posse has found a way to help colleges identify and nurture students who are likely to succeed in all conventional measures of success—college GPA, extracurricular involvement, and post-graduate attainment—students they otherwise would likely have missed.

To this end, with a $1.9 million grant received from the Andrew W. Mellon Foundation in 1999, Posse has developed a college-admissions assessment tool known as the Bial-Dale Adaptability Index, cocreated by Posse Foundation founder Debbie Bial. BDI is designed to identify students with specific leadership traits such as social interactions skills and the ability to work in groups that predict their ability to succeed in college and become active members of their campuses. BDI evaluates students in groups of ten or twelve at a time through exercises such as the "Lego test," in which members study a robot built of Lego blocks and then try to reconstruct it based on sharing their collective memories. Observers watch students taking the Lego test—as well as engaging in other dynamic interactions, such as running impromptu discussions on genetic testing or creating a public service announcement—to see who takes initiative, who collaborates well, and who is persistent.[1]

By scoring and tracking hundreds of New York City high school seniors who have applied to college through the Posse program, the study found that BDI can in fact predict these attributes in students: persistence, ability to access resources, and ability to contribute to a campus community (leadership).[2] After controlling for SAT scores, the study found that students with a high BDI were more likely to graduate in four years than were low-BDI students, and that high-BDI students had considerably higher GPAs than low-BDI students (again controlling for SAT scores). In fact, students' SAT scores had very little correlation with their BDI scores, and the former did not reflect the likelihood of success in school or graduation rates. Moreover, BDI students were shown to graduate at rates similar to those of the overall student body, despite having much lower SAT scores. BDI was found to be a particularly strong outcome predictor for black students, in contrast to standardized tests, which are even weaker predictors of black students' success than white students'.

Ultimately, the Posse program has the promise to realize its goal of being "a catalyst for increased individual and community development." Mike Schoenfeld was the dean of admissions when Middlebury first decided to partner with The Posse Foundation. Noting Middlebury's location in Vermont—"The whitest state in the nation," as Schoenfeld describes it—he initially sought to connect with Posse as a way to recruit more African American students to campus. However, he quickly learned that the program had more to offer. "Posse has influenced decision making in respect to who we think merits education," he says. "After ten years of success [with Posse], we looked to see what these students are doing. They rose to leadership roles and formed new clubs, and that is merit. They would go on extraordinary service trips to do things across the country, and that's merit. They would go work for Teach For America, and that's merit. What's more important: someone with all As or someone with some Bs who goes out and makes a difference in the world?"

CHAPTER SIX

Democratic Merit in the Classroom: Eric Mazur and Uri Treisman

YOU'VE READ HERE about the problems of testocratic merit—and there are plenty of them. It all begins with an admissions test, the SAT, that colleges use to select the "best and the brightest." The so-called best and the brightest are often nothing more than students who can perform well on a test, often by using quick strategic guessing with less-than-perfect information. Boys, for example, do better on the math portion of the SAT than girls. They routinely score forty to fifty points higher. Many people say, "Well, that's because girls are ignored in high school math." That may be true, yet despite their lower SAT math scores, these girls do just as well as the boys when they take math courses in college. The difference becomes evident when you interview students as to how they approach the SAT. The boys basically view it as a pinball machine: the goal is speed and winning. The girls, on the other hand, want to work through the problems before they put down the answer. For the SAT-test defenders, carefully analyzing a question, apparently, does not exemplify merit. Our over-emphasis on the testocracy has us confusing merit with speed and the confidence to guess.

How to guess is one of the topics covered for students whose families can afford intensive and expensive test preparation and training. This economic division, combined with the fact that the SAT is normed to the values and culture of the upper-middle class, allows certain demographics to replicate their success. Yet these same test defenders ignore the fact that the SAT is a poor predictor of academic performance over four years. As I noted in the example of the Yale class of 2009 "By the Numbers" chart, the emphasis on tests is so great that by the time students have graduated from college, their SAT scores are often still their most valued trait. For this cohort, it's unclear what the "value-added" of the college experience has been, since they have already been ranked and sorted in the admissions process like contestants in a beauty contest. The result is a pyramid-shaped meritocracy where everyone competes for the few spots at the very top. Affirmative action falls short as a complete solution because it simply repopulates this hierarchy, allowing it to persist.

This hierarchy under which our educational system currently operates—which sees merit as individualistic, measured by tests, and divorced from the notion of the collective good—poses several problems. It allows us to become comfortable seeing the success of a few at the top as proof of success of the group as a whole. The goal becomes moving a select few individuals to the very top, rather than preparing every student for future success. A meritocratic hierarchy based on individualistic notions of success also renders irrelevant how those at the top leverage their success: whether they lift up the whole group or only look out for "number one." The testocratic meritocracy blinds us to the fact that in the pyramidal structure most students necessarily will be at the bottom. Though a few students can leverage the system by capitalizing on their socioeconomic class to perform well on the SAT and then win admission to elite institutions, most students remain untouched by current "solutions." Society as a whole loses by embracing a system that focuses on and rewards the lucky few, while leaving out the unfortunate many.

Despite living in a testocratic world, some educators take approaches that seek to build from the bottom up. They are constructing a concept of democratic merit that is interdependent because it advances, furthers, and supports the achievement of the group as a whole. It makes an oval-shaped meritocracy, rather than a triangle-shaped one. Everyone benefits.

I have seen the benefits of democratic merit firsthand. At Harvard, the final exam for my Law and the Political Process class permits but does not require small groups of students to volunteer to work together in teams of three or four. Working in teams generates confidence and, most important, bolsters students' understanding of the assigned reading over the semester. It goes back to my own experience as a voting rights lawyer. Often, we worked in teams. As members of a group of lawyers, we had read the same cases but had different interpretations of those cases. It was very helpful to have to deal with those alternative interpretations rather than just assuming that your interpretation is right and you can charge ahead in a straight line. So much of the way law school works is in opposition to the reality of how one actually works on a case: the professor does all the talking and then (in the case of some of the research findings) about 10 percent of the class occupies 40 percent of the rest of the class time. Most of that 10 percent are men, which means there aren't too many other men speaking and certainly very few women.

My students have an option to work in a group or work individually for the final—and it's important to say that the exam is not predictive. I've seen some group finals that are not very good and some individual finals that are terrific. It's not as if I'm going to give more credit to a group final than to an individual final. But I see a final exam as a learning opportunity rather than just a judging opportunity. Working with two or three other people is a more creative way to complete a final because you have to explain why you're doing X or Y so it makes sense to your colleagues. In the process, your colleagues may give you feedback that can refine and expand your thinking.

I want to share the stories of two educators who use collaboration as a teaching tool. In their classrooms, learning takes place between and among students, rather than exclusively within the individual. The education of one necessarily means the education of another, as they go through the process together. All benefit from the learning of others through these constant processes of joining minds, ideas, and ways of thinking. Considered in this way, it is no surprise that the pedagogical approach of these two educators has proven highly successful.

The first educator, Eric Mazur, a physics professor at Harvard University, uses a peer-to-peer, or peer-instruction-based, instructional model. Rather than listen passively to a lecture, students in his course work together to solve both conceptual and complex problems. The second educator, Uri Treisman, while teaching mathematics at the University of California at Berkeley (he is now a professor at the University of Texas), organized students into "calculus clubs" through an initiative he created called the Emerging Scholars Program (ESP). With both teachers, students at both the high and low end of the grading curve achieve stronger learning outcomes. All students perform better, and learning is enhanced at the individual level, regardless of the student's initial ability. At the same time, disparities between groups—in Mazur's classroom, between male and female students, and in Treisman's, between African American and Asian students—have been almost completely eliminated. This is no small feat, since these differences have persisted for as long as most of us can remember.

ERIC MAZUR'S STUDENTS start class differently from most other science majors and pre-meds at Harvard. Instead of sitting back, taking notes, and listening to the professor drone on, they begin the day with a quiz. Not the type of quiz that matters in the way most do but a quiz intended to stimulate discussion among the kids in the classroom. It's never graded. It's only one question long. And its sole purpose is to generate heated debate between and among students, rather than to rank and sort them in a pyramidal hierarchy, or for one or more of them to try to impress the professor.

Mazur is a typical Ivy League professor—he's middle-aged, buried in his research, and has taught the same course for years and years—but he had an epiphany almost two decades ago. He had been teaching introductory physics at Harvard and was doing great at it: his students were performing well on tests; he was getting rave reviews, including Teacher of the Year awards; and majors in the field were moving on smoothly to the next courses in certain tracked sequences. Yet despite all this, he felt that something was not right. Often, students would score high on tough exams but then give responses to questions in class or on a test that suggested a serious lack of understanding of the core concepts underlying the material. He realized that his apparent success had given him a false sense of satisfaction. Yes, his students could "plug and chug" answers on an exam—take new numbers and use a known formula on a familiar problem that mirrored one in their textbook—but did they really understand physics at a deeper level?

The answer, Mazur believed, was no. Students were not grasping the core concepts of the subject; they understood exactly and only what he had told them during the lecture, which took up the entire sixty-minute course period three times a week. Mazur was puzzled at this realization. How was it that he had won all these awards, followed exactly the instructional model he'd been taught, had some students regularly score close to perfect on the exams, and yet many students still weren't learning? Once he thought about this conundrum a bit, it actually started to make sense. Students listened to him recite formulas, memorized them, and then reproduced his methods. They never had to really rethink problems or have them make sense on their own terms, so of course they didn't grasp concepts in a deeper way.

The problem was that most students only engaged with the material by themselves and through the professor. They never had to explain it to someone else, which meant they never had to really think about the concepts. So they memorized the formulas, familiarized themselves with the standard formats for questions, and got really good at solving problems that matched ones they had already seen. In short, they learned how to take a test, at the expense of actually learning how to use the assignments to solve real-world problems.

Mazur stepped back. What was his part in the students' learning process that was not delivering real results? The instructional format he used was not one he had created; indeed it is by far the most common format to follow both for science and nonscience college courses around the country. But it had made his students dependent on him and the lecture notes he would distribute. They never figured things out on their own, or with each other, for that matter. They were intensely focused on *him*. They had been trained to think that *he* possessed and had the power to convey all of the knowledge. Mazur was the "sage on the stage." If he did not lecture or hand out his notes one day, what would his students do? He decided it was time to find out.

Starting in the fall of 1990, Mazur developed and instituted a model he now calls "peer instruction." The model works as follows: Mazur gives students a prompt—a conceptual, big-picture question—based on the reading of the previous night. He asks students to think about their response for a minute and then pick the answer they think is right. Everyone has a clicker, and although the results are anonymous, they are displayed on a screen for everyone to see. For example, the screen will show that 30 percent of students chose response A, 20 percent response B, and so on. Next, students are told to "convince their neighbor" that their answer was correct. At this point, the classroom lights up. Students who in any other science classroom would likely be sitting silently, listening, and perhaps absorbing now actively engage in the teaching of their peers. Each student is paired randomly with just one neighbor, who may have chosen the same or a different answer. The two classmates debate and attempt to reach a consensus on the correct response within the two minutes or so that Mazur gives them. After the time is up, Mazur refocuses the class attention to the PowerPoint display. "What do we think now?" he asks. He puts up the same question on the screen and again asks students to anonymously record their answers using a clicker. Overwhelmingly, students get the answer right this time around. Within just two minutes, students get a concept and really know it. As Mazur says, the power of logic prevails.

This sequence of learning is known as "think-pair-share." Once the process is complete, then Mazur engages in "teaching"—meaning he gives an explanation of the correct answer—but only briefly. The exciting thing for the class is when he asks the new question. The class is now on the edge of their seats and remains so for the entire period, waiting for question after question, when they can not only figure out the answers but also convince their classmates. Though the prompts generally target core concepts rather than complex mathematical formulas, Mazur manages to get in a few of those questions as well.

The ratio of professor-student talking and listening is now reversed. Whereas Mazur used to spend almost the entire period talking, and students used to spend almost the entire time silent, the class rhythm now beats to a different drum. Lectures have become virtually obsolete in his classroom. Yet despite Mazur's more muted presence, he finds his value as a teacher is higher. By creating the prompts in a classroom structure that facilitates collaboration, students actually learn better.

Mazur knows this because he is a meticulous record keeper. He has recorded students' test scores since he began teaching introductory physics in 1985, and he has kept detailed track of final grades. Year after year, scores fell along almost an identical curve. Some students scored at the very top, many in the middle range, and a portion at the bottom: it was predictable. When Mazur saw the scores of the first class taught with peer instruction, he was floored. Scores had gone up at the top and bottom of the curve, both for complex problems and for core concept ones. The achievement gap narrowed, toppling the typical cluster of isolated high achievers at the top of the pyramid. Perhaps most notably, the disparity between men's and women's scores disappeared in his class. This disparity had persisted throughout his decades of teaching and it persists in most college physics classrooms across the country today. He had been stumped by it and resigned to feel that it was beyond his control. Yet with the introduction of the peer-instruction method, the sexes were performing both equally well and better. And they were for once actually getting the concepts, not just plugging and chugging answers.

Mazur has continued to use this method for more than two decades; he has exported it to physics professors at other colleges and universities, including junior colleges. The incredibly positive results persist across the board. Achievement gaps among groups narrow, and all scores go up. Why does this fairly simple method seem to work so well? Mazur thinks it's in part because it makes students think and reason like the new learners of the material they are. As a result, they are better teachers to each other. They can connect with their classmates in a way that Mazur cannot, because concepts are so ingrained in his mind and his way of thinking. In short, he can no longer remember the mental links it took to get there. Students are better at that; they are academically there with each other.

This collaboration has other benefits. Working with peers energizes all students to engage and ensures that the education of each and every one is accounted for. No one gets left behind. In the lecture setting, students who did not understand were left to their own devices. Now they can benefit from the different perspectives of their peers. And this doesn't shortchange learning, because the power of logic prevails: the best argument to fit the facts wins. The concepts become more understandable to those who aren't catching on, and those who are catching on learn more themselves by teaching it.

The class style of Eric Mazur's classroom has changed from that of an orchestra, where each student is assigned his or her own music, to a jazz band, where communication inspires enhanced performance in the moment. This rhythmic difference translates to a material difference as the achievement gap within Mazur's classroom is greatly narrowed, moving more toward the oval-shaped concept of democratic merit and away from the triangle-shaped testocratic one.

PROFESSOR MAZUR IS NOT the only university lecturer who has come to dislike the "plug and chug" approach to teaching. Three thousand miles away, at the University of California at Berkeley, Uri Treisman was having the same realization at about the same time. Treisman was comfortable as a graduate student teaching in the Department of Mathematics, but he was becoming uncomfortable with the persistent achievement gap between African American and Asian American students in his classroom. He set out to identify what he might be doing wrong, embarking on a journey that would point him to a similar destination as Mazur's: collaboration.

For Treisman, the numbers just didn't add up—and he had developed a career out of making sense of numbers. In the mid-1970s, 60 percent of black or Latino students at Berkeley who completed first-term freshman calculus scored a D or an F.[1] Faculty members blamed the low passing rate on a variety of factors outside the university's control: lack of student motivation, inadequate preparation, lack of family support, or a student's low-income background.[2] Yet the data negated these explanations. Black students with high SAT-math test scores performed more poorly in their first-year calculus courses than did black students with median math scores.[3] So, inadequate preparation wasn't the problem. Furthermore, black students from lower-income brackets performed better in calculus than those from more affluent backgrounds, disproving the theory that socioeconomic background was the driving culprit.[4] Finally, interviews illustrated that blacks accepted into a top-tier university like UC Berkeley were highly motivated and enjoyed extensive family support.[5]

Treisman searched for a resolution to this conundrum. What he discovered led to a redesigned calculus curriculum that embodies the core components of democratic merit: peer collaboration, social support networks, and higher-level problem solving. Called the Emerging Scholars Program, it has had stunning results. Before the implementation of ESP, only 22 percent of black students received As or Bs.[6] This number jumped to 54 percent among ESP participants.[7] ESP's effects were most striking among black students scoring in the top third of the SAT: only 28 percent of those in traditional sections got As or Bs, while 71 percent of those in ESP earned As or Bs.[8]

How did Treisman achieve these results? He knew something was awry. The same black students who were getting Fs in calculus were getting As in their "Study Skills" class.[9] Treisman observed that both Asian and black students were minorities at UC Berkeley, yet Asian calculus students consistently outperformed their black peers. The nagging question was why. When Treisman looked beyond student test scores and toward student behavior, he had his breakthrough. Treisman realized he needed to know more about student study habits. He turned to his video camera.

Treisman selected twenty of the highest-achieving calculus students of Chinese heritage, and twenty of the lowest-achieving calculus students of African or African American heritage. He then used a film crew to videotape these two groups of students over the next four months. In Treisman's own words, he and his crew "decided to literally move in with the students and to video tape them at work. We wanted to understand what was going on when they studied calculus [and] got stuck on problems."[10] When filming was complete, Treisman and his colleagues journeyed up to Lake Tahoe to analyze hundreds of hours of unedited videotapes. The footage revealed a compelling difference between the two cohorts: the African American students studied in complete isolation, while the Asian American students formed study groups.

Treisman summed up the findings of the footage:

What did studying mathematics mean for Black and Chinese students? For the Black students it meant this: You wake up in the morning. You go to class. You take notes. You get your homework assignment. You go home. You do your homework religiously and hand in every assignment on time. You put in six or eight hours a week of studying for a calculus course, just what the teacher says, and what happens to you? You fail. An important point here is that the Black students typically worked alone. Indeed 18 of the 20 students never studied with their classmates. . . .

What about the Chinese students? They studied calculus for about 14 hours a week. They would put in 8 to 10 hours working alone. In the evenings, they would get together. They might make a meal together and then sit and eat or go over the homework assignment. They would check each other's answers and each other's English. . . . They would edit one another's solutions. . . . They had constructed something like a truly academic fraternity, not the more typical fraternity: Sigma Phi Nothing.[11]

Thus, the videos revealed that doing your homework religiously was not enough. Putting in the recommended hours of studying was not enough. Completing every assignment was not enough. What was? True mastery of the material developed out of structured conversations about calculus with classmates.

Just as Eric Mazur at Harvard had witnessed, the footage illuminated the various benefits of studying in collaboration rather than in isolation. The Asian American students worked through difficult problems together. They taught each other mathematical shortcuts and alternative strategies for attacking tough problems.[12] If a problem was still difficult for the entire group, they would identify it as "one of the instructor's 'killers.'" They then felt comfortable approaching the professor for help, since the problem had posed a dilemma for all their peers.[13] These peer networks created a secure learning environment where students questioned and taught one another and helped develop the confidence of all the learners.

After analyzing the videotapes, Treisman understood that black students did not lack motivation but rather were missing out on a collaborative approach to studying that would help them excel. Until college, most black students had relied upon solitary study as a strategy for academic advancement. This is how you did it if you came from schools where your peers devalued scholastic success. To fit in with your group and avoid ridicule, you might pretend you didn't study, and then achieve in private. Isolation was a strategic advantage rather than a flaw.[14]

But college calculus was different. Calculus demanded that students develop problem-solving skills and higher-level conceptual thinking. Students needed to learn how to approach problems from multiple perspectives, how to identify misunderstandings, and how to find creative solutions. As shown in the video footage, these skills were best achieved by working interactively with peers on difficult problems.[15]

Students made the mistake of worrying about their final test grade rather than the process by which they learned the material. Treisman set out to change this, so that the constant student question would no longer be "Will it be on the test?" Instead, he wanted students to become excited about collaborating on challenging problems. The program's goal was "not merely helping students pass calculus . . . but, rather, producing mathematicians."[16]

With that goal in mind, Treisman designed ESP, which author Tina Rosenberg has described as a collection of "calculus clubs."[17] ESP differs structurally from "traditional" calculus courses in three key ways. First, Treisman extended the course requirements from four hours to six hours. At the same time, he created interracial study groups, which challenged both the black students as well as the rural white students to excel. He makes it clear that ESP is not a remedial program but rather a highly rigorous program of study.[18] Second, the workshops reject the classic lecture model in favor of peer-to-peer teaching.[19] Teaching assistants (TAs) monitor the classroom while students work through difficult math worksheets in small groups. When students get stuck, they ask each other questions and solicit help from their peers before receiving a helpful suggestion from the TA. Third, the workshop model explicitly teaches students to value their peer network; they have a responsibility to their peers to attend classes, prepare each night's assignments so they can discuss their findings in class, and spend some of their time collaborating with classmates to solve math problems.[20] In ESP's opening orientation, Treisman persuaded students "that success in college would require them to work with their peers, to create for themselves a community based on shared intellectual interests and common professional aims."[21]

Rosenberg said that the peer-to-peer feature of Treisman's classroom is more than just an example of collaboration; it is actually a rare example of *positive* peer pressure in which students are pushed by their friendship to change their work habits. Treisman expanded the cohort of students who were naturally working together to include the entire class—creating a larger "club," in Rosenberg's words—and was then able to take advantage of peer pressure. In many important ways, peers are better educators than teachers. As Rosenberg notes, "Peer pressure changes you, and in turn you change a community, a bureaucracy, a culture, a government—a world."[22]

These changes certainly transformed Treisman's calculus classroom. "A visitor to a workshop session might initially mistake it for a noisy study hall," he says. "But after a few moments the impression of disorder evaporates, and the purposeful nature of the activities becomes clear: the leader is circulating unobtrusively, alert to the dynamics of the clusters of students, all of whom are wrestling with a set of problems on a worksheet."[23]

The program trained students to work together so that they could "alternate giving and receiving assistance." Such group work did not always come naturally, as Treisman explained: "Students are responsible for critiquing one another's work . . . but as they continue, they learn to question and to demand explanations. Then they are more ready as well to defend their own ideas."[24] In Treisman's model, students learn how to articulate their own insights and learn from others'.

Treisman is a numbers guy through and through, and the numbers assured him that his model was effective. He found that black and Latino participants substantially outperformed not only their minority peers in the traditional courses but also their white and Asian classmates with the same incoming test scores. Black students with math SAT scores in the low 600s were performing comparably to white and Asian students whose math SATs were in the mid-700s. Treisman also proudly related that "many of the students from these early workshops have gone on to become physicians, scientists, and engineers. One Black woman became a Rhodes scholar, and many others have won distinguished graduate fellowships."[25] Follow-up studies have confirmed that the ESP model benefits all students, although the greatest gains occur among underrepresented minorities.

Treisman has developed a pedagogical formula that works: initially the numbers didn't add up for Treisman, but his calculus clubs now show, both through numbers and personal testimony, that a student's performance in calculus is not predetermined by his or her incoming math SAT score, nor by his or her race. Instead, all students will reach higher levels of mastery—both individually and as a group—when the classroom becomes a collaborative space for peers to work together by sharing different strategies, perspectives, and approaches.

THESE CLASSROOM INNOVATIONS show that it is possible to transform our vision of merit from a testocratic one to an interdependent, democratic one. We can change the culture of the classroom from test-oriented lectures to a collaborative atmosphere that teaches our students how to problem solve. Teachers can create learning environments where students work to understand the material together, and through this process, the goals of learning become shared. Teachers can also reward the ability to work in groups, which is perhaps the crucial skill for solving the complex problems of the twenty-first century. Students who are better skilled at working with and learning from others are better poised to listen, to communicate, and to lead, and this structure encourages students to cultivate collaborative skills. This is Malcolm Gladwell's Marine Corps approach to education, which assumes that all students have the capacity to perform. In Mazur's and Treisman's classrooms, the class-wide improvement is evidence enough of this. When we topple the pyramidal structure of testocratic merit, students learn better, they learn how to problem solve more generally, and, perhaps most important, they learn that their success is the success of the group, be it the classroom, the community, the country, or the world.

CHAPTER SEVEN

Six Ways of Looking at Democratic Merit

MAZUR AND TREISMAN offer striking stories of transformation. The structure of the classroom has been transformed, as have student interactions and individual achievement. It is impressive to learn that all students improved their test scores after Mazur and Treisman introduced collaborative-learning models. But it is perhaps more striking still to view these transformations together and realize that Mazur and Treisman have created something larger: a classroom culture shift. This culture shift affects students both internally, in how they define their values, and externally, in how they interact with peers.

Internally, Mazur and Treisman encourage students to redefine their personal understandings of intelligence and merit. They reject the dominant narrative about intelligence: that it is fixed, inherent, and measured by tests. Instead, Mazur and Treisman teach students to view intelligence as malleable and based on success in collaborative work. "Intelligence" is more expansive than a raw test score, and "merit" encompasses positive character traits such as communication, collaboration, and group leadership. Mazur and Treisman deliberately design lectures and classroom activities to persuade students about two key ideas: that intelligence involves hard work, yes, and that intelligence also involves interpersonal skills. Intelligence, in a democratic and meritocratic context, is never static.

The second shift in Mazur's and Treisman's classrooms involves external relationships. These professors encourage students to redefine their relationships with each other. Instead of working alone, students are encouraged to work together. Students become teachers and teammates. Classes show students that diverse perspectives can collectively lead to better solutions. Competition is replaced with collaboration: rather than focusing on their own isolated intelligence, students began to value and seek out new peer perspectives and partnerships.

These internal and external transformations shift the classroom culture toward a celebration of democratic merit. But observing this change is just the starting point. My question is how. How did Mazur's and Treisman's practices produce such results?

The world of social science helps us answer the question of what leads to success. Here I want to present six thinkers, six different researchers who approach this question from different angles. Carol Dweck and Paul Tough take up the question on an individual level by asking, What mind-sets, behaviors, and attitudes will lead to one individual's success and another's failure? The research of Anita Woolley and Scott Page addresses the question at a group level: How can a particular group achieve higher results than either other groups or individuals working on their own? Marilynn Brewer has looked at how the intersection between the individual and the group affects success. And, finally, Jo Boaler has explored an example of these successful approaches in the math classrooms of an urban public high school. Each of these thinkers casts light on a different dimension of how a culture shift can occur in classrooms like Mazur's and Treisman's and, perhaps most important, how we can spread these culture shifts to new people and places.

HOW DID MAZUR and Treisman change student test scores? Research suggests that test scores improved because a fundamental change was at work: a shift in mind-set. Both Mazur and Treisman decided to change how they spoke about "answers": they encouraged students to value the learning process, not just the final score. By changing the values in the classroom, Mazur and Treisman worked to redefine the measures of merit.

Both Mazur and Treisman taught students that their aim was not to get the "right answer." Instead, the goal was to understand how to get to the right answer. Students needed to explain their approach to a problem and articulate any obstacles they encountered. These professors made it clear that students should not be embarrassed if they gave a wrong answer or had no answer at all. Students were urged to view giving wrong answers as an opportunity for higher understanding. They needed to embrace their struggle so that they could understand their missteps and learn better, alternative approaches. In this way, Mazur and Treisman rejected the concept that merit is defined by a final test score. Instead, they each rebuilt the platform of a meritocracy, using Amartya Sen's concept of merit. They redefined merit as an opportunity for both continual self-improvement and self-reflection, as well as the development of collaborative approaches that stimulate learning.

After creating a system that values learning processes over right answers, both Mazur and Treisman witnessed a rise in their students' test scores. Why would a pedagogy that values self-improvement over test scores yield an increase in student performance?

Dweck and Tough may have the answer. In their work, these researchers set forth to answer the puzzling question: Why do some children succeed while others lose their way? Dweck, a psychology professor at Stanford University, has approached this problem by designing tests to measure patterns of student motivation. Tough, a writer interested in educational reform, has approached the puzzling question by looking at methods that enable low-income children to reach higher levels of success.

Though their methods vary, Dweck and Tough have reached similar conclusions. They both found that children will be more successful if they believe their intelligence is capable of growth, rather than believing intelligence is innate. Tough has added to Dweck's observations by concluding that a child will also be more successful if she or he focuses on building character strengths in a similar way, viewing them as malleable rather than fixed. Understanding Dweck's and Tough's conclusions allow for a better understanding of why Mazur and Treisman were so effective when they changed the curricular culture in the classroom.

CAROL DWECK'S NUMEROUS studies show that an individual who believes intelligence is "fixed" is much more likely to fail in the face of new challenges, while an individual who believes that intelligence can grow with hard work is much more likely to excel in the face of new challenges.

Dweck first investigated the underpinnings of human motivation as a graduate student at Yale University in the 1960s.[1] She had read about "learned helplessness" in animals. Psychologists at the University of Pennsylvania showed that after repeated failures to stop something negative from happening, most animals conclude that the situation is hopeless and beyond their control. After such an experience, the animal often remains passive even when it can effect change, a state the researchers called "learned helplessness."[2]

After reading these studies, Dweck observed that some people also exhibited "helplessness" in the face of repeated failure. But she was more fascinated by the people who don't—the people who still persevere in the face of setbacks. She wondered: "Why do some students give up when they encounter difficulty, whereas others who are no more skilled continue to strive and learn?"[3] After more than three decades of conducting countless studies, she concludes that "one answer . . . [lies] in people's beliefs about why they had failed."[4] In short, students who attribute poor performance to a lack of innate ability will continue to perform poorly. However, students with the same incoming abilities who believe their poor performance is due to effort—and thus can be overcome with hard work—will improve their performance over time.[5]

Dweck has developed a broader theory of what separates the two general classes of learners: helpless versus mastery oriented. Through her research, she found that students not only diverge in how they explain their failures but that they also hold different "theories" of intelligence. Some subscribe to a "fixed mind-set" of intelligence, others to a "growth mind-set."

Dweck coined the term "fixed mind-set" to describe "the helpless ones [who] believe that intelligence is a fixed trait: you only have a certain amount, and that's that. . . . Mistakes crack their self-confidence because they attribute errors to lack of ability, which they feel powerless to change."[6] Students with a "fixed mind-set" avoid challenges because they want to avoid mistakes.[7] They spend their time documenting their intelligence or talents instead of developing them.[8] In contrast, students with a "growth mind-set" believe that intelligence can be developed through education and hard work. "They want to learn above all else," Dweck writes. "[Since] slipups stem from a lack of effort, not ability, they can be remedied by more effort. Challenges are energizing rather than intimidating; they offer opportunities to learn."[9] To illustrate the behavior of "growth mind-set" students, Dweck shared several anecdotes from her studies:

> [Growth-minded students] focused on fixing errors and honing their skills. One advised himself: "I should slow down and try to figure this out." Two schoolchildren were particularly inspiring. One, in the wake of difficulty, pulled up his chair, rubbed his hands together, smacked his lips and said, "I love a challenge!" The other, also confronting the hard problems, looked up at the experimenter and approvingly declared, "I was hoping this would be informative!"

Dweck wanted to know whether a growth mind-set led to higher, lower, or equal levels of student performance. To answer this question, Dweck did what she was trained to do: she designed an experimental study, and then another, and then another. All the results repeatedly reaffirmed her conclusion that students with a growth mind-set have greater academic success and are more likely to outperform their fixed-mind-set counterparts. For example, in 2007, Dweck and her colleagues shared the results of a two-year study that monitored 373 students during the transition from elementary to junior high school, when classwork gets more difficult. At the beginning of seventh grade, all the students had roughly the same incoming math scores. But though students had equivalent scores, they did not have equivalent mind-sets—some saw intelligence as fixed, while others believed it could "grow" with effort. To assess these students' initial mind-sets, Dweck and her colleagues asked students at the start of seventh grade to agree or disagree with statements such as "Your intelligence is something very basic about you that you can't really change." After determining each student's initial mind-set, Dweck and her colleagues tracked each student's grades. The results? Not only did students with "growth mind-sets" perform better on math tests than their fixed-mind-set peers, but this difference in performance also grew over time.[10]

Furthermore, Dweck's research finds that even our "mind-set" is not innate but malleable. The type of praise an individual receives can affect an individual's mind-set. When students receive praise for their intelligence, they are more likely to adopt a fixed mind-set than when they receive pats on the back for effort. In a 1998 study, Dweck found that those who were congratulated for their intelligence

> shied away from a challenging assignment . . . far more than the kids applauded for their effort. . . . When we gave everyone hard problems anyway, those praised for being smart became discouraged, doubting their ability. And their scores, even on the easier problem set we gave them afterward, declined as compared with their previous results on equivalent problems. In contrast, students praised for their effort did not lose confidence when faced with the harder questions, and their performance improved markedly on the easier problems that followed.[11]

Dweck's studies show us two things. First, students who view intelligence as capable of growth will perform better than those who don't—that is, valuing the learning process over a test score will help students achieve at higher levels. Second, students are more likely to adopt a growth mind-set if others praise them for their effort rather than their intelligence. These conclusions mirror the results of Mazur and Treisman, who in effect increased student test scores by adopting strategies that promoted a growth mind-set over a fixed mind-set in their classrooms. As if they had been reading Dweck's work, both Mazur and Treisman placed great value on the learning process, not just on giving a right answer.

BUT THIS IS not the end of the story. Mazur and Treisman did more than just convey to students that intelligence was malleable rather than fixed. They also conveyed that success depended on certain study habits and behaviors that were—like intelligence—capable of improvement.

This focus on academic behaviors, or "character traits," may be another secret to student success, according to author Paul Tough. Like Dweck, Tough is interested in what makes some students succeed while others flounder. He decided to write a book that would help him "solve some of the most pervasive mysteries of life: who succeeds and who fails? Why do some children thrive while others lose their way? And what can any of us do to steer an individual child—or a whole generation of children—away from failure and toward success?"

His research question was similar to Dweck's. But while Dweck turned to social science for the answer, Tough decided to take a more holistic approach by showing the connections between very different fields of research: economics, neuroscience, pediatrics, and psychology. Surveying these various fields, Tough made a bold observation: the prevailing "cognitive hypothesis" that saturates our culture is misguided.[12] This hypothesis, he explains, is "the belief, rarely expressed aloud but commonly held nonetheless, that success today depends primarily on cognitive skills—the kind of intelligence that gets measured on IQ tests, including the abilities to recognize letters and words, to calculate, to detect patterns."[13]

This hypothesis is exactly what gives the SAT and other standardized tests their life's breath. Being able to half-decipher the meaning of an arcane word or to eliminate one or two wrong math answers and thereby improve one's ability to guess—without knowing how one has arrived at the right answer—these are the skills that our culture prizes. Yet the research and testimony that Tough encountered thoroughly discredit this "cognitive hypothesis." In its place, he has developed a new theory based on the importance of positive character traits. Tough found that what matters most to a child's success is not how much information we can stuff into a child's brain but rather "whether we are able to help her develop a very different set of qualities, a list that includes persistence, self-control, curiosity, conscientiousness, grit, and self-confidence."[14] Thus, Tough appropriately titled his book *How Children Succeed: Grit, Curiosity, and the Power of Hidden Character.*

Tough offers many studies and programs to support his assertion that success depends upon developing key character traits more than on simply developing rote skills. To show that IQ scores don't summarize intelligence, he gives the example of the Perry Preschool project, conducted in the 1960s. In this research project, children were recruited from a low-income neighborhood. Half were admitted to Perry, a high-quality, two-year preschool program, while the other half served as the "control group" without a free offer of preschool. The researchers followed the two groups of children for decades to track the effects of the preschool program. The results were not what you might expect. Researchers found that attending Perry Preschool had no lasting effect on the children's IQ scores. By third grade, both the Perry children and the control group had equivalent IQ scores. Researchers did observe, however, that attending Perry Preschool carried an important long-term effect. Compared to the control group, Perry students were more likely to have graduated from high school, more likely to be employed by age twenty-seven, more likely to be earning more than $25,000 a year by age forty, less likely ever to have been arrested, and less likely to have spent time on welfare.[15]

These results intrigued James Heckman, a professor of economics, who dug deeper into the archives. Heckman found that the Perry Preschool scored students on what Heckman called "noncognitive skills," such as curiosity, relationships with fellow students, social fluidity, and self-control. Heckman found that these noncognitive factors were responsible for as much as two-thirds of the total benefit that Perry gave its students and led, from his perspective, to the differences in measurable life outcomes.

From the Perry Preschool study, Tough concluded that social skills "and the underlying traits they reflected turned out to be very valuable indeed."[16] Tough has been able to show that character traits are important not only in an early childhood environment but in a college context as well. In his chapter "How to Build Character," he writes about David Levin, a founder of KIPP Academy. KIPP (which stands for the Knowledge Is Power Program) is an innovative charter school program whose mission is to provide a high-quality middle school education to children from low-income communities. Since its start in the 1990s, KIPP schools have yielded some highly impressive student scores. In 1999, the students of KIPP Academy in Bronx, New York, earned the highest scores of any school in the Bronx and the fifth-highest in all of New York City.

But Levin came to the same conclusion I am advocating in this book: test scores in and of themselves, as a single-minded approach to education, are meaningless. The initial cohort of KIPP in New York City did extremely well in terms of their test scores. They left middle school with outstanding academic results and most won admission to highly selective private or Catholic high schools. Almost every member of the Bronx class made it through high school, and most enrolled in college. But once in college KIPP students started to struggle: six years after their high school graduation, only 21 percent of the cohort had completed a four-year college degree.[17]

Levin was pained by this low graduation rate. He analyzed the dropout reports and noticed something curious: the students who succeeded in college were not necessarily those who had tested well or excelled academically in KIPP. Instead, they seemed to be the ones who possessed certain other gifts, skills like optimism and resilience and social agility. Levin knew then that he had to promote these traits among his students.

Levin worked closely with social psychologists Martin Seligman and Angela Duckworth to identify key character traits that would enable students to reach the highest levels of success, both in KIPP and later in college. After much discussion, they identified seven traits: grit, self-control, zest, social intelligence, gratitude, optimism, and curiosity. After identifying the traits, Duckworth worked with Levin to develop an evaluation tool that teachers and students could use to assess "character strengths." Then, in 2007, Levin introduced the first-ever "character report card." He knew there would be problems with quantifying character, so he asked students to rate themselves, as well as having teachers rate them. By 2011, Tough observed that the emphasis on character traits had gone "viral"—it was everywhere at the KIPP Academy in New York. Levin explains that the focus on character "has to permeate everything in the school, from the language people use, to lesson plans, to how people are rewarded and recognized, to signs on the wall. If it's not woven into the DNA of an institution, it will have minimal impact." Indeed, KIPP's increased emphasis on character has shown promising results. Though the first cohort of graduates was in 2003, all the academies, across the United States, saw only a 21 percent college graduation rate in six years. However, the class of 2005 doubled this graduation rate: 46 percent of KIPP students graduated in six years.[18]

The effectiveness of KIPP's character-building approach will become more apparent with time, but this example highlights the importance of developing particular traits in order to excel in college and beyond: resilience, optimism, and social agility. These traits are important not only for low-income students but for all students; they are essential ingredients for success. But the prevailing focus on test scores downplays the importance of these character traits—and it is the students who suffer the most because of it. Emphasizing an individual test score discourages students from taking risks, engaging in creative solutions, and embracing failure as an opportunity for learning.

Dominic Randolph, the headmaster of the prestigious Riverdale Country School, a prep school in New York City, shares the same concerns about the importance of teaching students character traits such as resilience and curiosity. Despite the different demographics of KIPP Academy in the Bronx and Riverdale (whose students primarily come from wealthy and highly educated families), Randolph worries that Riverdale students are missing out on strengthening their character, by which he means developing traits like grit and self-control that will carry a student through struggles and failure. He criticizes the over-emphasis on IQ testing, observing that "this push on tests . . . is missing out on some serious parts of what it means to be a successful human."[19] According to Randolph, a culture that focuses primarily on test scores fails to develop these critical character traits in its young people. It does not encourage students to take risks, develop curiosity, or engage in activities that may lead to failure and thereby growth. He explains, "People who have an easy time of things, who get 800s on their SAT's, I worry that those people get feedback that everything they're doing is great. And I think as a result, we are actually setting them up for long-term failure. When that person suddenly has to face up to a difficult moment, then I think they're screwed, to be honest. I don't think they've grown the capacities to be able to handle that."[20]

Unfortunately, Randolph's worries don't seem that far-fetched. I have already pointed out that the job choices of many graduates from our most elite colleges show a lack of empathy and creativity. In fact, the negative social repercussions of raising a generation of graduates afraid of bold pursuits that require some degree of struggle and potential failure could in the long run be devastating. In Tough's closing chapter, he observes: "There are fewer entrepreneurs graduating from our best colleges these days: fewer iconoclasts, fewer artists, fewer everything, in fact, except investment bankers and management consultants. Recently, the *New York Times* reported that . . . more than half of the [Princeton] class was going into investment banking or consulting—and this after the near-collapse of the finance industry in 2008."[21] James Kwak, an economics blogger and law professor, explained this trend toward banking and consulting among graduates of elite schools: "It's that the firms make the path and the decision so easy to take and so hard to resist."[22] Kwak concludes, "For people who don't know how to get a job in the open economy and who have ended each phase of their lives by taking a test to do the most prestigious thing possible in the next phase, all of this comes naturally."[23] A decline in creative leadership and problem solving is one possible side effect of emphasizing test scores over character traits like resilience, social intelligence, and curiosity.

The twenty-first century needs college graduates who can address the prevailing issues of our era, such as global warming, an expanding technological landscape, and the equitable distribution of opportunities. These issues require collaboration, experimentation, creativity, and optimistic perseverance; this kind of thinking will help us tackle old problems in ways that will provide us with new solutions.

MAZUR AND TREISMAN encouraged their students to value the learning process over a right answer. They emphasized the importance of openly discussing failures to move toward solutions, creatively approaching a problem by experimenting with different approaches, and recognizing that struggle was the only path to improvement. These principles fostered within students character traits such as resilience, optimism, and grit that often led to success. The development of these traits may partially explain why the students in Mazur's and Treisman's classrooms were far more successful at the end of the semester. It may also explain why Treisman's students were more likely to concentrate in mathematics as their college major and more likely to participate in, and lead, activities throughout the campus community.

But the transformations in our students are not only internal. We can also effect an external transformation that encourages student collaboration and interdependent learning—the roots of democratic merit. Research sheds light on how student collaboration can substantially improve overall performance when students teach each other, learn from one another, and value differing perspectives. However, the research also shows that performance does not automatically improve if people are put in groups; group dynamics matter. Our next four thinkers: Anita Woolley, Scott Page, Marilynn Brewer, and Jo Boaler help explain the dynamics that enabled the collaborations in Mazur's and Treisman's classrooms to be so effective.

ANITA WOOLLEY STUDIES INTELLIGENCE. She's a professor at Carnegie Mellon University in the department of cognitive science, a discipline that studies how the mind works. Woolley, however, is unlike most of her colleagues. Instead of studying the brains of individuals, she studies the "brains" of groups. Intelligence, for Woolley, is measured by the ability of groups. She calls this "collective intelligence."

In today's world, it is increasingly common for groups, rather than individuals on their own, to solve complex problems. A huge part of the reason for this is the complexity of the problems themselves. The world is getting more and more multidimensional, and it is virtually impossible for any one person to understand all the sides of a problem. People need to work together. Businesses organize themselves into teams to come up with marketing strategies. Government officials meet to devise national security plans. Scientists share information across large networks to develop new vaccines. In today's world, almost everyone is collaborating.

In a collaborative society like ours, measuring intelligence only in individual people—as cognitive scientists have traditionally done—seems to miss the point. Woolley has believed this from the start of her career. When everyone's working together, we should be concerned about how and why groups become smart. It makes little sense to focus so much on the intelligence level of the individual when most knowledge building and problem solving today happens within teams. Woolley wanted to delve deeper into what accounts for collective intelligence.

In beginning this endeavor, Woolley first asked, are groups smartest when they are made up of the smartest members? So, if we wanted to put together the brightest group, the one that would be the most effective at solving the problems of, say, government, or business, or science, would we simply try to find the smartest individuals and bring them together? This is a logical and traditional belief about group intelligence: throw the smartest people you can find into a room, and they're bound to be smart together.

Woolley set out to determine whether this widely held belief was true. She put together different combinations of individuals with varying IQ levels, genders, backgrounds, and so forth, and asked them to perform a variety of tasks: some simple, some hard. The groups worked away. In observing them as they worked, Woolley noticed that the groups acted very differently from one another. In some groups, everyone spoke and was encouraged to share ideas. In others, one or two people dominated the conversation. Each came to have a culture of its own.

By the end of the experiment, the performance of the groups varied dramatically. Some were very adept at solving all sorts of problems and tasks; some were not adept at all, and others were somewhere in between. In short, some teams were smarter than others. But why? Was it simply as everyone had believed, that the smartest groups were the ones with the smartest members?

What Woolley found was striking. The cumulative intelligence of the groups' members—if you were to add up the IQs of everyone in the group—was not predictive at all of the intelligence of the group as a whole. It didn't seem to matter whether the group was made up of the smartest individuals or of the least smart individuals. What mattered, instead, were a whole host of other factors.

Surprisingly, Woolley found that the sex of the members (largely because of that the group's internal social dynamics) made a huge difference on the outcomes. Groups with higher percentages of women performed better than groups with higher percentages of men. The "female effect," Woolley found, can be partly explained by women's tendency toward greater social sensitivities. Women were more likely to read nonverbal cues and perceive accurately what others were feeling or thinking. They were also more likely to encourage turn-taking in the discussions. The cooperation that women fostered led groups to take advantage of the skills and knowledge of all the members. Those attributes were brought out and shared, and then multiplied, in a way that didn't happen in groups with more men and less cooperation. Communication and inclusivity were key to the groups' success—far more so than the overall intelligence of the members.

Woolley's findings were consistent with other research that's been done on the role of gender in group processes. In a study of groups working in business settings, Graham Fenwick and Derrick Neal found that groups with equal numbers of men and women, and/or with higher numbers of women than men, performed better than groups with higher proportions of men.[24] The reason for this, they found—as did Woolley—was the positive effect women had on the ability of the group to collaborate. The presence of women was shown to encourage and facilitate group processes so that all members felt comfortable participating and sharing their knowledge and skills.

The consequences of Woolley's findings are huge, with implications for business, government, and the sciences. With so much happening in groups, as it does in today's world, Woolley's work suggests that our efforts would be better directed toward building group intelligence. Group or "collective" intelligence is not simply a direct outgrowth of individual intelligence. Rather, it grows and develops in unique ways that have to do with social sensitivities, group norms, and internal team dynamics. Efforts to improve productivity, efficiency, or creativity should involve teams with a high proportion of women and be structured to encourage inclusive, participatory group norms.

For education, the findings are even more significant. They suggest that our heavy focus on building individual abilities—as measured so carefully in our testocratic world—might be misplaced. Rather than focusing excessively on enhancing individual IQs, as today's educational system does, we need to improve—and reward—students' abilities to work in groups. This is the challenge we must meet if we want to prepare our next generation to solve the complex problems of today's and tomorrow's worlds.

ACROSS THE COUNTRY from Anita Woolley, Scott Page came to a similar realization in his research: the highest-performing group was not composed of the highest-performing individuals. While Woolley uncovered the importance of female participation to group success, Page uncovered the importance of diversity, where "diversity" refers not to what we look like on the outside but to our distinct tools and abilities. In his book *The Difference: How the Power of Diversity Creates Better Groups, Firms, Schools, and Societies*, Page recounts that he "stumbled upon" the power of diversity.[25] This happened during his "first real job," as an assistant professor of economics at the California Institute of Technology in Pasadena.

The year was 1995. At the time, Page had no intention of building his career around mathematical models of diversity. He was simply enjoying the fact that he could wear shorts to work every day, while exploring Caltech's abundant resources. Page did have a budding interest in how groups performed as problem solvers. Like other economists, Page had made two observations. First, he saw that our modern world demanded complex problem solving to contend with multidimensional issues like addressing environmental policies, designing social welfare systems, and cracking secret codes. Second, he saw that groups were more adept than individuals at solving these multidimensional problems. However, Page had not yet explored what types of groups were the "best" problem solvers.

One winter evening, Page decided to have what he describes as "a little fun." He constructed "a computing model of diverse problem solvers confronting a difficult problem." To create "groups," Page selected members from a pool of problem solvers who had received different test scores on an assessment. He formed two different types of groups: one of "high performers" and the other a "diverse" group of problem solvers. The "highest performers" group comprised members with the highest test scores. The second, "diverse" group was made up of a random sampling of members with a range of test scores: some high, some low. These varying test scores reflected what Page called different "tools," or ways of thinking—a fascinating way of looking at democratic merit. Page then created a mathematical formula to test each group's ability to solve difficult problems. From this model, Page observed that the random sampling of diverse performers outperformed the highest performers every single time.

This may sound counterintuitive. You mean the brightest don't always do the best? In Page's model, diversity trumped ability. In truth, Page said, he was startled by his own finding. And he wanted an explanation. So he partnered with his colleague Lu Hong to try to explain this surprising discovery. Unlike Woolley, in her social science study, Page and Hong used a different method of proof: mathematical formulas. They showed that the "highest performers" possessed the same "tools" for, or approaches to, problem solving, whereas individuals who received a range of scores exhibited different tools or approaches. A group would be most successful when its members could share their diverse approaches to a problem.[26] Through his study, Page built upon the saying "two heads are better than one" to show that two heads with diverse approaches will outperform two heads with the same approach but higher test scores.

Page points out one of the limits of his finding: diverse groups will only outperform homogeneous groups if the members share their different approaches with one another. A group's social dynamics are relevant; witness studies such as Woolley's, which focus on how group norms affect performance. But Page's research is also important because it demonstrates why our society should promote diversity for reasons besides "fairness." Today's world demands problem solvers. Groups outperform individuals in problem solving, and Page shows that diverse groups—with diverse approaches—will yield the best solutions to modern dilemmas.

IN ADDITION TO wanting to be "ourselves" as individuals, humans want to be part of groups. This desire takes on many different forms. We organize into families, communities, countries, nationalities, and ethnicities. As we come to see ourselves as part of these groups, we adopt a number of different "social identities." Every day, people identify themselves by referencing their membership in all sorts of groups—by gender, ethnicity, college alma mater, hometown, participation in a club or activity. The list goes on. What these different group-based identities reflect is the desire to "belong" or to feel part of a group, and one aspect of group-belonging that people particularly like is how belonging to a certain group makes them different from members of other groups. While being part of a group means that you share things in common with fellow members, it also means that those things make you stand out. For example, sports fans both love their team and their fellow fans *and* think that their team's rivals and *their* fans are despicable. Red Sox fans both love other Red Sox fans and hate Yankee fans.

So what does this have to do with education? Well, as it turns out, how much you perceive your membership in the "in-group"—whether you're a Red Sox fan living among other fans in Boston or alone in Yankee territory—affects your performance. If you perceive yourself as part of the in-group, and if that in-group is high performing, then you are more likely to perform well, just because you are part of that group. Alternatively, if you perceive yourself as outside the in-group that performs well, or if you perceive yourself as part of a group that is low performing, you are more likely to do poorly.

Marilynn Brewer, a social psychologist at Ohio State University, calls this idea "optimal distinctiveness." Optimal distinctiveness means that not only do individuals want to belong to a group, but they also care about how unique they are simply because they are a member of this group. People seek group membership, and also group differentiation. That's why Red Sox fans care not only about the Red Sox and being part of their fan base but also about how they're different from the Yankees and their fan base.

Research shows that belonging in groups, as well as being differentiated by groups, influences the way people think about themselves. When people are members of groups, they start to define themselves in the terms of the group. They also start to shift their concerns and motivations from themselves as individuals to the group as a whole. The relevance of all of this for education is that students' self-identification as members of high-performing or low-performing groups actually affects their own, individual performance. When students see themselves as part of a high-performing group—for example, a particular ethnic group, some defined "talented" group within the school, or the like—they are more likely to perceive themselves as high-performing and then to actually do well. Conversely, if the student perceives herself as a member of a "low-performing" group, she is more likely to perceive herself as a low-performing student, and then actually perform worse. This middle step—where individuals see themselves as having the characteristics of the group of which they are a part—is essentially self-stereotyping. And what the research shows is that it actually leads to behavior that confirms the stereotype.

Furthermore, research that Brewer and others have done shows that when conceptions of self change—when people start to see themselves as members of groups and evaluate their success on this ground—their ideas about what might be their duty to others shifts. This effect is particularly pronounced in high-performing groups. When individuals are in the high-performing in-group category, they not only perform better, but they also "develop a cooperative orientation toward shared problems."[27] In a classroom setting, this means that when students see themselves as part of the in-group, and that group is high performing, they tend to care more about problems that are shared by the whole group.

Thinking back to Mazur's and Treisman's classrooms, Brewer's theory has a lot of relevance. Essentially, most of what Mazur and Treisman do is to create a classroom setting that treats all students as possessing "merit" and as being capable of succeeding. In short, they make everyone part of the in-group. All students perceive themselves as part of the group that is high performing and develop collaborative attitudes that foster even greater success than had they been working on their own. It's not surprising, then, that not only do those individuals succeed, as the studies show, but they also develop mind-sets that facilitate cooperation and help each other develop shared learning goals—which raises the tide for all.

—m—

FOR THOSE OF YOU who may wonder if the work of Mazur and Treisman is applicable to K–12 teaching, Stanford University professor Jo Boaler's research of the Railside School offers one such example.[28] Railside is a public high school in the Bay Area of California, considered to be on "the wrong side of the railroad tracks."[29] Students come from homes with few financial resources, and many are English-language learners. Yet in Boaler's five-year longitudinal research, students in Railside's high school math program outperformed the nearby school's wealthier students on standardized tests, even though Railside students entered as ninth graders performing far below the comparison students on those tests. Not only did Railside students achieve greater mathematical gains, but more of them enrolled in higher-level math courses and enjoyed math more. The achievement gap between students from the "better" side of the tracks was greatly narrowed. Students also gained what Boaler calls "relational equity," which means they learned to collaborate by valuing the ethnic, gender, and social-class diversity of their peers. The success of Railside provides a perfect example of the concepts I've discussed in this chapter: the power of a growth mind-set, the dynamic impact of teamwork, and the value of drawing from diversity.

In her research, Boaler studied three California high schools: Railside, Greendale, and Hilltop. Railside's student body was 40 percent Latino, 20 percent African American, 20 percent white, and 20 percent Asian Pacific Islanders; 30 percent of students qualified for free or reduced lunch. Greendale had a predominantly white student body (90 percent) and low poverty rates (only 10 percent qualified for free or reduced lunch). At Hilltop, a rural high school with a student body that was 60 percent white and 40 percent Latino, 20 percent of their students qualified for free or reduced lunch. Another useful statistic to note is that 30 percent of the students at Railside were English-language learners, whereas no students at Greendale and only 20 percent of Hilltop's students were.[30]

Boaler studied approximately three hundred students in "traditional" math classes at Greendale and Hilltop and approximately three hundred students in "reform oriented"[31] math classes at Railside in a four-year study, following their progress from ninth through twelfth grades. When the study began, ninth graders entering Railside tested well below the performance of Greendale and Hilltop students. At the end of the first year of the study Railside students had approached the test scores of Greendale and Hilltop students. By the end of the second year, Railside students had significantly outperformed Greendale and Hilltop students.[32] At the end of the third year, Railside students continued to outperform Greendale and Hilltop students, although not to a statistically significant degree.[33] At the end of the fourth year, achievement tests were not administered because a more selective group of students remained in math classes in all three schools.[34] Nonetheless, in this fourth year of the study, the twelfth grade students at Railside were enrolled in advanced math classes at a much higher rate (41 percent of students) than were the students at the other two schools (27 percent).[35] Railside students also enjoyed math more, with 71 percent responding positively on a second-year questionnaire, compared to 46 percent of Greendale and Hilltop students.[36] What made this stunning achievement possible, especially given the ninth graders' lower entering test scores and the untracked classrooms? Teachers at Railside engaged in the same practices as Mazur and Treisman yet for younger learners: developing a growth mind-set, working in collaborative groups, and using diversity as an asset for achievement.

To begin with, Railside did not engage in the tracking practices typical of most high schools, where students are slotted into remedial, regular, or honors-level math courses that predetermine and restrict their educational opportunities both during and after high school. At Railside, all entering ninth graders were assigned to algebra. Interestingly, the Railside students who benefited the most from this untracked heterogeneous approach were the students who tested highest when entering the ninth grade—which should alleviate concerns that these students would be "held back" by their peers who didn't test as well as they did on the math assessments.[37]

Next, teachers at Railside maintained high expectations of their students and offered them challenging tasks—all the while emphasizing the importance of effort over ability and continually reminding students that they could accomplish anything if they put in the effort.[38] This message was internalized by students at Railside. In the words of Sara, a ninth grader:

> To be successful in math you really have to just, like, put your mind to it and keep on trying—because math is all about trying. It's kind of a hard subject because it involves many things. [. . .] But as long as you keep on trying and don't give up, then you know that you can do it.[39]

Railside teachers taught their students not only that they must persist in the face of struggle but also how—by using "multiple-ability treatments."[40] Multiple-ability treatments emphasize the importance of multiple abilities required for a task. When beginning an activity, Railside teachers would discuss with students the multiple abilities necessary to complete the group task (for example, reasoning, creativity, spatial-visual reasoning) and told students, "None of us has all these abilities; each one of us has some of these abilities."[41] Instead, students were told they needed to work together to accomplish their math tasks. Throughout the students' four years at high school, teachers continued to remind them of the importance of effort and persistence for success in math class. This was mainly done through teachers' emphasis on collaborative group work.

How does this group work operate? Analyzing six hundred hours of classroom-observation video, collected throughout the study, Boaler found that Railside students worked in small groups 72 percent of the time and presented to the class 9 percent of the time. Only 4 percent of class time was spent with teachers lecturing to students, with 9 percent of class time spent questioning students as a whole class. In stark contrast, in the traditional classrooms at Greendale and Hilltop, 21 percent of class time was spent lecturing, 15 percent questioning students as a whole class, while 48 percent of the time students worked individually in their books, and only for 0.2 percent of the time did students present to the class.[42] Writes Boaler:

> Enhanced student participation had a purpose of course. Rather than the learning by rote which was occurring in the traditional classrooms of Greendale and Hilltop, students at Railside were expected to justify their reasoning, which not only improved their mathematics understanding but also created respect for each other. A 9th grader, Jasmine, explained the multiple approaches of her math class and the expectation of justification by saying, "It's not just one way to do it [. . .] It's more interpretive. It's not just one answer. There's more than one way to get it. And then it's like: "Why does it work?"[43]

At Railside, students were expected to justify their reasoning for their answers and to question each other. Teachers emphasized their expectation that students take collective responsibility for their group. To do so, students were taught about positive teamwork through "complex instruction," a group-work strategy that incorporates roles (for example, team captain, facilitator, recorder reporter, resource manager).[44] Teaching students how to collaborate in groups not only benefited student learning, but it also facilitated respect for the diversity of the range of strengths that students brought to the group. Interviews with Railside students highlight the respect that students had for each other and the responsibility they took for both their own and their group's learning.

> INTERVIEWER: Do you prefer to work alone or in groups?
> AMADO (Year 1): I think it'd be in groups, 'cause I want, like, people that doesn't know how to understand it, I want to help them. And I want to—I want them to be good at it. And I want them to understand how to do the math that we do.

LATISHA (Year 3): It's good working in groups because everybody else in the group can learn with you, so if someone doesn't understand—like, if I don't understand but the other person does understand, they can explain it to me, or vice versa, and I think it's cool.

ZANE (Year 2): Everybody in there is at a different level. But what makes the class good is that everybody's at different levels, so everybody's constantly teaching each other and helping each other out.[45]

Railside students did not refer to classmates as "slow" or "dumb," as they did at Greendale and Hilltop. Rather they referred to some students as those who "don't do their work."[46] This highlights students' internalization of a growth mind-set, where effort rather than ability determines success in mathematics. What is perhaps most interesting about this heterogeneous and group approach is that not only did students achieve greater mathematical gains, but the achievement gap was narrowed, and students learned to value each other's ethnic and cultural backgrounds, the "relational equity" I mentioned.

Just as Scott Page showed that a diversity of students produced the best solutions, the students at Railside benefited from the diversity of their classrooms. Because students were not tracked into ability groups, math classes were diverse both in the different academic strengths that students brought to the classroom and also in the ethnic diversity of the student body—40 percent Latino, 20 percent African American, 20 percent white, and 20 percent Asian–Pacific Islanders. When teachers emphasized the importance of growth mind-sets, collaborative group work, and multiple perspectives, students learned that success in math comes from applying these principles. This is illustrated in this interview with Ayanna and Estelle, Railside seniors in the fourth year of the study.

INTERVIEWER: What do you guys think it takes to be successful in math?

AYANNA: Being able to work with other people.

ESTELLE: Be open-minded, listen to everybody's ideas.

AYANNA: You have to hear other people's opinions, 'cause you might be wrong.

ESTELLE: You might be wrong 'cause there's lots of different ways to work everything out.

AYANNA: 'Cause everyone has a different way of doing things, you can always find different ways to work something out, to find something out.

ESTELLE: Someone always comes up with a way to do it. We're always like, "Oh, my gosh, I can't believe you would think of something like that."[47]

Boaler proposes that this "relational equity," where students treat each other respectfully and fairly consider each other's diverse perspectives, should be one of the goals of education. She argues that schools should "produce citizens who treat each other with respect, who value the contributions of others with whom they interact, irrespective of their race, class or gender, and who act with a sense of justice in considering the needs of others in society."[48] At Railside, as students learned to value multiple and diverse perspectives in the classroom, they also came to value the ethnic and cultural diversity of their classmates. Students' work in collaborative groups at Railside influenced their social relationships, as illustrated by this interview with Robert and Jon, also seniors in the fourth year of the study.

ROBERT: I love this school, you know? There are schools that are within a mile of us that are completely different—they're broken up into their race cliques and things like that. And at this school, everyone's accepted as a person, and they're not looked at by the color of their skin.

INTERVIEWER: Does the math approach help that, or is it a whole school influence?

JON: The groups in math help to bring kids together.

ROBERT: Yeah. When you switch groups, that helps you to mingle with more people than if you're just sitting in a set seating chart where you're only exposed to the people that are sitting around you, and you don't know the people on the other side of the room. In math you have to talk; you have to voice if you don't know or voice what you're learning.[49]

Students in the diverse classrooms of Railside had higher mathematics gains, outperformed the students of Greendale and Hilltop, enjoyed mathematics, and enrolled in advanced math courses. The achievement gap among ethnic groups either narrowed or disappeared.[50] By contrast, achievement disparities by ethnic group at the traditional Greendale and Hilltop schools remained throughout the five years of the study.

Railside is not the only school engaging in this approach. The San Francisco Unified School District, for example, is currently in its fifth year of a professional development initiative in which middle and high school math teachers throughout the district participate in a thirty-hour summer course, meet throughout the year, review student work, and watch videos of each other's instruction. Just as teamwork is expected of students, math teachers in these cities also work in teams. In Seattle, former Railside teacher and current University of Washington research associate Lisa Jilk coaches math teachers' implementation of the "complex instruction" approach in Seattle public schools. At Vanguard High School, a public school in New York City in which most students qualify for free or reduced-priced lunches, math teachers meet weekly to support each other's use of group work with their diverse students in the school's untracked, heterogeneous math classes.

RAILSIDE AND OTHER urban public schools in San Francisco, Seattle, and New York City serve as enlightening and hopeful K–12 examples of the same culture shift advocated at the university level by Mazur and Treisman. Through collaboration and innovative approaches that allow students to value effort over ability, each of these examples follows the research of Dweck and Tough in promoting a growth mind-set rather than a fixed mind-set. By learning how to work productively in diverse groups, the shift in student perceptions on subjects such as intelligence results in greater learning gains, positive attitudes, and students' appreciation of the diversity of their peers. This echoes both Woolley's research on turn taking, social sensitivity, and the role of women, and Page's research on the value of diversity in groups and multiple perspectives. This is democratic merit in action—and what could be the beginning of a widespread culture shift that will ultimately benefit both individuals and society as a whole.

CHAPTER EIGHT

Democratic Merit in a Twenty-First-Century World

TIME AND AGAIN I find myself returning to Amartya Sen's definition of merit as an incentive system that rewards the actions a society values. As I have argued throughout part 2, a shift from honoring testocratic merit toward democratic merit produces a variety of benefits aligned with the values our culture professes: students display a higher capacity to problem solve, a greater demonstration of both leadership and peer collaboration, and an increase in fairness. As the title of part 2 indicates, these are the "solutions"—but their impact does not end in the field of education. They also carry a heightened significance: a culture shift, from testocratic to democratic merit, can translate into benefits for our whole society. Returning to Professor David Labaree's observation: America has always conceptualized education as a training ground for tomorrow's citizens, leaders, and professionals. Increasing collaborative skills in a classroom can—as these students graduate and enter the workforce—reverberate throughout society by increasing collaborative skills in the workplace.

Thus, I'd like to go a step further in considering how a shift toward democratic merit can not only positively affect our classrooms but also positively affect our societal institutions and governance. There are strong indications—through anecdotal and empirical evidence—that the skill sets promoted by systems of democratic merit will better serve the challenges of a twenty-first-century world, which demands complex problem solving and collaboration among diverse individuals. Indeed, it is becoming increasingly apparent to today's business leaders and politicians that increased collaboration—rather than pure competition—is what will lead to greater outcomes.

I want to offer two examples that illustrate how both the professional and political sectors can benefit from graduates who know how to collaborate, problem solve, and embrace a diversity of perspectives. First, I'll consider the story of Atul Gawande, who demonstrates how collaboration can improve health-care quality in this country while decreasing its spiraling costs. I will then turn to Archon Fung's study of how cross-collaboration can lead to better governance and legal solutions. Both of these stories shed light on how a shift toward democratic merit is not only ideal but also necessary to move us forward into the demands of a twenty-first-century world.

BY TRAINING, ATUL Gawande is an endocrine surgeon. He has a reputation in the operating room for being bold, innovative, and detail oriented. Colleagues will attest that Gawande is known for being a self-professed rock 'n' roll fanatic who listens to artists like David Bowie while performing surgery,[1] for encouraging doctors to collectively engage in constant self-reflection, and for meticulously following checklists during procedures.

However, it is Gawande's work outside the operating room that illustrates the potential power of a culture shift toward democratic merit. Gawande is also a prolific writer. In numerous opinion pieces, articles, and books, he has explored the best practices in medicine in order to suggest improvements in the medical industry. In 2009, Gawande decided to take on a major issue preoccupying Washington, DC: how to bring health-care costs under control. In tackling this issue, Gawande highlighted how cultures of collaboration and communication can lead us to better solutions.

In Gawande's words: "The explosive trend in American medical costs seems to have occurred here in an especially intense form."[2] According to a 2008 World Health Organization report, the United States spent more on health care per person than any other country in the world. WHO also found that the United States spent the highest percent of its gross domestic product on health care. Of course, none of this would be a problem if more expensive health care translated into better health care. Unfortunately, most studies have found that having the world's highest health-care costs do not result in the United States having the world's best health-care system. In fact, the 2000 WHO report ranked the United States thirty-seventh in health care, behind nations like Morocco, Cyprus, and Costa Rica.[3] In 2007, the Commonwealth Fund did a study that looked at health care in Australia, Canada, Germany, New Zealand, the United Kingdom, and the United States. Their report ranked the United States last or next to last in four out of five criteria, including quality, efficiency, and access.[4]

Gawande observed that rising costs were leaving countless individuals uninsured or drowning in medical debt. Just as important, high costs were also "devouring our government."[5] He recognized President Barack Obama's concern that "the greatest threat to America's fiscal health is not Social Security. . . . It's not the investments that we've made to rescue our economy during this crisis. By a wide margin, the biggest threat to our nation's balance sheet is the skyrocketing cost of health care. It's not even close."[6] Gawande decided to search for solutions, and he uncovered a possible answer to efficiently curb costs while enhancing care: greater collaboration between medical providers. Gawande would publish these findings in a 2009 New Yorker article "The Cost Conundrum," which gained attention from readers across the country, including President Obama.

That year, Gawande's questions about health-care spending brought him to McAllen, Texas. McAllen calls itself the Square Dance Capital of the World, but it has another reputation: it's one of the most expensive health-care markets in the country. The only city that outspends McAllen on per person health-care costs is Miami, which has much higher labor and living costs. Gawande interviewed businessmen, hospital administrators, and doctors in McAllen and neighboring counties, and various theories were offered to explain why, for example, McAllen's Medicare costs were twice the national average.[7] Some residents hypothesized that McAllen's population was not healthy and, therefore, required higher spending. But Gawande disproved this theory by finding that cities comparable to McAllen in terms of demographics, such as El Paso, were no more healthy and yet spent much less on health care.[8] Others suggested that McAllen's health care must be superior to that of other regions. However, there was no indication that the city's services produced better outcomes than those of neighboring cities, like El Paso. But Gawande concluded that McAllen's higher costs did not correlate with higher quality, noting, "Medicare ranks hospitals on twenty-five metrics of care. On all but two of these, McAllen's five largest hospitals performed worse, on average, than El Paso's. McAllen costs Medicare seven thousand dollars more per person each year than does the average city in America. But not, so far as one can tell, because it's delivering better health care."[9]

Instead, Gawande found a different explanation for the higher costs in McAllen: professional culture. The hospitals that drove up spending costs did not provide better care. They simply had medical practitioners who were driven by profit and competitive self-interest. In contrast, institutions like the Mayo Clinic, which provide higher-quality care and lower costs, exhibit a different culture: collaboration among practitioners.

Gawande suddenly became less interested in the problems of McAllen and more interested in how the Mayo Clinic built a culture that produced one of the highest-quality, lowest-cost health-care systems in the country. The Mayo Clinic implemented two noteworthy practices. First, it discouraged competition by pooling all the money received by doctors and the hospital system. Doctors instead received a salary. CEO Denis Cortese explained that this payment reorganization occurred so that "the doctors' goal in patient care couldn't be increasing their income." Unlike the doctors in McAllen, who aggressively competed with neighboring practitioners to maximize personal profit, Mayo Clinic doctors worked together to provide the best care for patients. To nurture this collaborative culture, the Mayo Clinic implemented a second important practice: staff members participated in team brainstorming sessions. Gawande observed that "the doctors and nurses, and even the janitors, sat in meetings almost weekly, working on ideas to make the service and the care better, not to get more money out of patients."[10] These two changes in industry practice were intended to produce better care for patients. The Mayo Clinic succeeded in this goal, and as an unintended side effect, it also produced society-wide benefits by lowering health-care costs.

Gawande pointed out that the Mayo Clinic story is not an aberration. Other hospitals have reached similar results when a culture of collaboration replaces a culture of profit-driven competition. For example, the health-care system in Grand Junction, Colorado, ranks among the highest in quality care providers and yet incurs among the lowest costs. Michael Pramenko, a doctor and medical leader in Grand Junction, explained that the rise in quality and fall in costs correlated with two changes. First, doctors agreed they would not compete over insurance providers but would instead universally agree on fees for all patients. This drove down costs. Second, practitioners agreed to meet regularly in small peer-review committees to go over their patient charts together. By increasing group problem solving, practice problems decreased and quality of care improved. Once again, the culture of collaboration over competition was a recipe for better outcomes, both for patients and for taxpayers.

The methods adopted by Mayo Clinic and Grand Junction to achieve better health-care outcomes are the same as those promoted by classrooms organized around democratic merit: a culture of collaboration rather than competition, a sharing of diverse perspectives, and increasing equity among colleagues. By promoting teamwork and collective problem solving, a culture shift toward democratic merit could drive us in the direction of solving health care's most pressing problems while also improving quality of care. That's just one way that workforce practices that encourage cross-collaboration and communication can lead to increased productivity and success in the twenty-first-century marketplace.

Embracing democratic merit over an obsession with testocratic merit and competition can have important implications not only in the world of business but also in how our society is governed. Recall David Labaree's observation that one of the purposes of a public education system in a democratic society is to prepare citizens to participate effectively and meaningfully in the processes that govern us. A healthy democracy depends on everyone having equal opportunity to understand and shape public action. When our education system produces a culture of competition instead of collaboration, or when it produces citizens who cannot work together to solve problems or incorporate diverse voices, this has important consequences for democracy. We have seen how individuals breaking out of their narrow roles to cooperate and experiment with others can make health care more effective, efficient, and individualized. An example of a similar innovation in local government can show how the culture shift that I propose can improve democracy more broadly.

Archon Fung is a political scientist who has taken a close look at how collaboration, experimentation, and diversity can best relate to the way we govern ourselves. His work is concerned with a simple question: how can we make our political institutions more democratic? To find an answer, he decided to look not at the highest levels of the political process but at a far more humble site: a network of community police and school boards established throughout Chicago in the mid-1990s.

Rather than leaving the supervision of schools and police to a central office, this innovative initiative gave the community a voice in managing these institutions.[11] For example, parents, teachers, students, and neighbors volunteered as members of a community board for their high school, meeting regularly to make decisions about personnel, budget, facilities, and curriculum. These boards were set up at the level of a single police beat or elementary school, a scale small enough that the most closely affected individuals could have a direct say. For instance, policing routinely involves discretion and local expertise on the part of individual officers. Rather than managing this discretion with one-size-fits-all policies designed by a central office, local boards allowed citizens to come together and direct police discretion toward problems that residents consider important.

Fung spent two years in Chicago, sitting in on these meetings, carefully observing how they worked, and also noting when they didn't. Because the boards in Chicago were set up on a small-enough scale for participants to focus on pragmatic solutions to specific problems, Fung labeled this model "street-level democracy." One of the hallmarks of street-level democracy is its openness; where the traditional democratic process expects participants to enter with their views determined by political commitments, street-level democracy allows residents to develop and clarify their thoughts on complex political matters through deliberation and experimentation. Fung describes how two people with completely different views on a political or cultural question are unlikely to find a way to work together in the typical political process. In the context of making the decisions that are necessary to making their neighborhood safer, however, they can easily work together to solve problems. Through that process, they can even learn to trust one another.

Fung explains how these collaborative or participatory models can produce better results than hierarchical, pyramid-like management structures. In fact, the Chicago initiative emerged from a belief that public services might be more effective if managed with direct input and participation from the people they serve. Though the centralized nature of large bureaucracies seems to promise coordination and efficiency, Chicago residents were frustrated that the city was failing to educate children and keep streets safe, especially in poorer communities. These large bureaucracies had originally grown as the problems we wanted government to address became more complex: whereas police had once focused simply on catching perpetrators of crime, we now also expect them to prevent crime, and we judge their performance based on the crime rate. As cities grew, pyramid-like bureaucracies seemed like the best way to manage complex functions like policing, education, and environmental control. But the more complex these functions became, the harder it was for bureaucracies to remain effective and equitable at the individual and local levels. It took toppling these pyramid-shaped hierarchies on their side in the form of street-level democracy to ensure that the complex problems of Chicago residents were dealt with in a way that remained effective.

Fung describes a neighborhood-policing board in Chicago's Rogers Park area. Residents of the neighborhood had noticed an increase in drug dealing, prostitution, and late-night noise on one particular street corner. After meeting to discuss the problem, residents learned that the landlord of a laundromat on the street corner had refused to renew the previous management's lease and instead had rented the laundromat to his son. Whereas the old management had tolerated drug activity, the son now took steps to discourage it, removing indoor pay phones and banning anyone involved with drug activity from the premises. As a result, drug dealers and their customers started congregating outside the laundromat and using outdoor pay phones across the street. Once the residents identified this source of the problem, they immediately took steps to fix it. First, they organized walking groups to create a positive community presence in the streets. Second, they approached the owner of the outdoor pay phones. When he agreed to remove the phones but learned he could not cancel his contract with the phone company, the community board pressured the company to at least block incoming calls from the phones. Rather than leaving this problem to some kind of centralized fix (such as the city removing all pay phones from street corners) or waiting for police to catch and arrest the criminals, residents developed a pragmatic solution, through trust, experimentation, and persistence.

Fung emphasizes that street-level democracy requires not just creating new political processes but also teaching the personal qualities that citizens need to productively collaborate and deliberate with their neighbors. If we want public education to prepare citizens who will participate more effectively in our democracy, then we need to ask if the values and skills our education system teaches actually nurture these qualities. Does lining everyone up according to achievement actually produce better citizens? How do we teach the next generation how to effectively collaborate and deliberate with others?

Fung offers another example that shows the importance of making decisions collaboratively: two residents of a neighborhood each faced problems they wanted the police to address. One lived by an open-air drug market and was worried about recent shootings there. The other lived in a wealthier part of the neighborhood and was concerned about teenagers drinking in the park by his house. Absent community policing, their best means of attracting attention or resources to either problem would probably have been for one of them to lobby more vocally than the other. In fact, even at a community meeting, the residents' instinct probably would have been to show up and make the loudest case for why his problem mattered more. But in a process that emphasizes individual collaboration and deliberation, the two residents simply shared and justified their concern to each other—as if they were talking through a physics or a math problem in a classroom, both trying to find the right answer. After a while, the resident from the wealthier neighborhood who was worried about underage drinking recognized that the shootings were a more pressing issue. Rather than competing, the residents collaborated.

Unfortunately, this is not how our democracy currently works. Nor does the meritocracy encourage this kind of thinking. Our political process allocates public resources through a kind of competition: individuals and groups act in their own rational self-interest, demanding the changes most important to them, and the loudest or most credentialed voices win. This is how defining "merit" narrowly and individualistically, rather than collectively, manifests itself in the political process. The problem isn't that the resident from the wealthier neighborhood was concerned with underage drinking because he didn't care about the issues his poorer neighbors faced; it was just that he was never asked to sincerely consider them. No part of the traditional democratic process asked him to empathize with the concerns of others or to compare his concern to other problems in the neighborhood. He only had to advocate for the problems he knew about. His role was to compete against his neighbors, not work with them.

Fung emphasizes the importance of another quality that our culture's current obsession with testocratic merit does not cultivate: a willingness to try fresh approaches knowing they might fail. Just as Mazur and Treisman found in their classrooms, Fung found that meetings were most effective when participants were open to changing their minds based on new arguments and evidence, rather than by being stubborn or dogmatic.

Fung further describes how this process of experimenting with and adapting solutions also resulted in participants feeling more invested in the outcomes. He tells the story of a crusty police officer who spends his days stopping suspicious-looking teenagers on the street, not because he is naive enough to believe this really improves safety but because he simply believes it's his job. Likewise, he attends the community policing program only because his job requires him to do it. When he learns at a meeting that these patrols anger residents, he cuts back on the practice to avoid controversy, earning a bit of their trust. Later, when residents tell him to focus on an area where they claim that criminal activity is occurring, he discovers two drug houses he never would have known about otherwise. With help from the residents, they evict the drug dealers.

On one level, this story is about how police improve their work by listening to the community. But Fung emphasizes another development: collaboration has changed how the police officer views his job. He now sees how his actions can actually make a difference. Before, he was just doing what he needed to do to get paid, regardless of whether it actually made a difference. But now he is starting to build an interest in seeing the neighborhood improve through his actions. Likewise, residents who previously only saw the police swooping into the neighborhood to harass people for no clear reason now recognize an opportunity to work with law enforcement, to limit damaging practices and encourage better ones.

Fung also looked at who exactly was doing all this participating. After all, just as our current political systems tend to reward those with more money or time to spare, Fung wondered if those same people also have more influence even in supposedly collaborative processes. Instead, he found that even in community groups that featured a range of economic or educational backgrounds, collaboration was possible once residents started thinking beyond their narrow self-interest. He studied a geographically and economically segregated police precinct, where median incomes on the east and west sides of commuter-rail tracks differed by almost $30,000. Because the tracks were such a solid physical barrier, the problems each side faced rarely spilled into the other. As such, residents had a clear interest in trying to secure more police resources for their own side. Yet they formed a board to deal with their problems. Fung noted that cynics might expect this board to not function productively, given residents' fundamentally contradictory interests and their initial inability to genuinely empathize with and incorporate the perspectives of others. Fung wondered if the wealthier residents would use their higher incomes, free time, education, civic skills, and institutional connections to dominate community meetings, as they can do with the traditional political process—or educational beauty contest.

Fung sat in meetings observing the group for its first ten months. He reports that, just as skeptics might suspect, the west side residents did initially have more influence in the meetings. During the first four months, the group set the community-policing agenda, with the more articulate and aggressive residents dominating the conversation. Though residents from the poorer east side continued to attend the meetings in equal numbers as their counterparts from the wealthier west side, they mostly kept quiet. For example, at one session, the meeting facilitator asked residents to propose "new business" for the meeting. When a police officer reported on multiple shootings on a particular street corner on the east side, the facilitator attempted to open the conversation up further by asking if anyone felt the corner was an ongoing problem. No resident answered, and no further action was planned. In comparison, west side residents had raised concerns about street peddlers and urged police to enforce vendor-license requirements more strictly. The police did, and the peddlers were gone within three months. The west side residents also raised concerns about traffic violations, such as drivers hopping curbs or cutting through traffic lights, and demanded a stop sign at a busy corner. The police promised to increase traffic surveillance at these spots, and the alderman's representative promised to request the stop sign.

Once again, the problem was not that west side residents were trying to shut out their east side neighbors. Rather, the group simply operated the way many groups do that lack the skills to work collaboratively; by default, their proceedings fall into the hands of those who can explain a problem the most articulately or aggressively.

Fortunately, this began to shift by the second half of Fung's time observing the group. Part of this was due to a change in procedure from a free-form town-hall-style format to a five-step process in which the group would (1) list problems and rank them according to priority; (2) gather all the information that different residents had about the problem; (3) figure out steps that residents, police, and other city workers would take to deal with the problem; (4) implement the strategy; and (5) evaluate how implementation went.

This structured, thoughtful, and open-ended approach to problem-solving echoes the kind of thinking that the creative educators I described earlier in the book are trying to teach, as well as the kinds of skills that innovations like performance-based assessments are designed to test and reward. Fung observed how it produced much better outcomes than when the group simply focused on whatever concerns were raised by the loudest or most articulate residents.

In the meeting that Fung observed, the idea for this structured problem-solving process came from a community organizer who had learned that the police issue "beat plans," ranking safety problems according to urgency. She thought these plans should be developed by residents, not police, and proposed that the group list problems and prioritize them. One resident mentioned a drug house on the west side of the neighborhood, and everyone quickly agreed this was the single most important safety issue for the group to address. Several months of meetings had been largely silent on this problem, and suddenly all participants, east and west, black and white, agreed it should be their biggest priority. Rather than each person ranking what was the most important to them or competing against one another, the group proceeded to allocate shared resources based on a consensus about what was most important for the community as a whole.

Fung also looked at areas with even more extreme poverty, to see whether street-level democracy could be effective even in these conditions. While one might expect that people with more free time and resources would be the ones who can afford to spend their evenings at meetings discussing crime, Fung found that residents from poorer neighborhoods and residents without college education actually participate at greater rates. Specifically, he explains that in two neighborhoods with identical crime rates, income levels, and racial compositions but different levels of college education or median income, the one with fewer college-educated residents or a lower median income was more likely to have better attendance at community meetings. Whereas our current meritocratic approach to politics bars people from having a meaningful say in public action unless they know how to compete with and outperform everyone around them, street-level democracy opens politics up to all kinds of perspectives and focuses these perspectives directly on solving the problems people care most about. Street-level democracy encourages citizens to listen to the perspectives of their neighbors and peers regardless of what credentials accompany those perspectives.

Chicago residents participated at these community meetings because they saw that their participation made better schools and safer neighborhoods possible. Rather than viewing themselves as passive consumers of public action that bureaucrats produce, collaboration encouraged and rewarded these citizens' direct civic engagement. Although the residents participating in these meetings had initially done a poor job of listening to others or working together, this improved once the city developed a curriculum to teach them problem solving and collaboration skills and when the groups turned to a process that was open-ended and valued diverse perspectives. Unfortunately, our education neither teaches nor rewards these skills, instead urging children to compete individualistically and narrowly to reach the top of a hierarchy. Just as the obsession with competition and individualistic merit begins in classrooms, so can a more effective democracy.

CONCLUSION

I HAVE BEEN at this a long time.

In 1966 (I realize I am dating myself!) I wrote the following letter to the College Board about what was then called the Scholastic Aptitude Test:

Gentlemen:

In regard to the December 3, 1966, SAT, two of the questions asked were rather ambiguous. I am referring to two questions on the Math Section which were part of the series of Data-Sufficiency Questions. Since this type of problem is an attempt to determine a student's power of logical analysis, information is given to answer the question without giving the student taking the test an opportunity to give the reasons for one's decision. I don't think that anyone who recognized implications in the questions should be penalized.

The two questions are as follows:

How many questions are there on a test?
a. Mary answered 15 questions correctly and received a mark of 30%.
b. John answered 35 questions correctly and received a mark of 70%.

Who has more US coins?
a. Pete has 24 cents and Ed has 26 cents.
b. One of Ed's coins is a quarter.

Superficial examination of these two questions leads one to the conclusion that sufficient information is given to answer the question. Closer analysis, however, leads one to the dilemma that re: ques. 1—we are assuming that each question is worth an equal number of points and we have not been given any evidence on which to base such an assumption and re: ques. 2—since we have been asked who has more US coins we do not have any information on whether any or all of Pete's coins are US coins or perhaps Canadian coins. A student can therefore come to the conclusion that there is insufficient data in both A and B of ques. 1 & 2 to answer the questions.

It is my humble opinion that to be fair to a student who is directed to focus on "sufficiency of data" two things should occur . . .

That was me as a sixteen-year-old. Look out world! I would like to point out that I had the restraint to wait two days after taking the SAT to write and mail the above letter. I don't think I ever got a response, but writing the letter was cathartic because it was annoying to have these questions that didn't make any sense.

When I got to Radcliffe College at Harvard University, the SAT followed me there. During one of our first conversations in our dorm room, my freshman-year roommate immediately explained that she was worried she would never get married because she would never find a man as smart as she was—after all she had perfect scores on the SAT! Even then the conflation of self-worth, or other-worth (in terms of who you wanted to spend the rest of your life with), with test scores struck me as odd.

Instinctively I sought out my posse of black women at Radcliffe. This was the 1960s, so there was a lot going on, not only in terms of the Vietnam War but also the civil rights movement. Martin Luther King Jr. was assassinated while I was in college. It was a very sad time, but it was also a very exciting time because students felt empowered to raise issues publicly without being considered dangerous. My posse wanted to express our concern that there were very few black women being admitted to Radcliffe. We sat in in the corridor leading up to the dean's office. We were told to be very "ladylike"; I remember well. This was our ladylike approach, but I think we got their attention. They certainly started admitting more students of color.

I graduated from college and then from law school, and early in my career I took a job as assistant counsel with the NAACP Legal Defense and Educational Fund, first in Washington, DC, when the Voting Rights Act of 1965 was amended and extended, and later in the New York City office, as head of the LDF Voting Rights group. That was my first experience in collaborating with coworkers in a way that the whole really was greater than the sum of its parts. We were a group of people who were committed to helping make a sustainable change, not just for blacks but also for Latinos and for poor people.

When I introduce my students to this environment now, I'm not trying to get them to support the NAACP Legal Defense Fund. What I want them to feel is what it is like to work with somebody else to change the status quo. You have to be very creative. You may get a sense of pride that you are actually making a change, but you aren't making it yourself; you are part of a group of people—some of whom are similarly situated, and some of whom are differentially situated, but all of whom have a common goal.

That's one of the reasons that I give students in my Law and the Political Process class the option of writing an exam in a group of two or three. People might say, well, that's ridiculous; that's just cheating. Those people most likely have never practiced law, because that's not my experience, for example, of how you write a brief. You don't just write it by yourself. Sometimes you do, but if you have someone with a slightly different perspective, it's very helpful. And it's not only the intellect that matters but also one's ability to implement ideas and commit to communicating one's perspective. That was one thing I loved about the women and men in the Legal Defense Fund. Whether they were black or white, they had been litigating cases for years, and when I joined them, they didn't hesitate to push me into the rotation with everybody else. We weren't going to specialize and inhabit our own individual silos—which would have been tempting for me as a black woman in the post Jim Crow–era when we worked in the South, in Arkansas, North Carolina, Alabama, or Louisiana. "Nope, Lani," they would tell me. "It's your turn to cross-examine the governor tomorrow. . . ."

When you actually practice as a lawyer, it isn't as if each member of a team is given one witness to prepare and questions him or her on the stand, and then that's the end of the conversation. Everybody works together. When we don't encourage collaboration and the whole host of complementary skills relevant to greater understanding, we lose out. Instead, we choose people who excel at the same, limited things; admit them to the best schools; and send them off to do their own individual work in their own individual careers. Testocratic, not democratic, merit. When you look closely, it's everywhere.

Yet there are visionaries out there, shifting our educational models from ones that favor testocratic merit to those that favor democratic merit; visionaries who approach the problem from many different vantage points. Some of them have transformed the classroom, where professors like Eric Mazur and Uri Treisman have created a culture of collaboration rather than competition. Some transformations have occurred on the campus, where The Posse Foundation has reimagined what a collective college admissions process could look like and identified students for their future leadership potential rather than their static, pre-existing test scores. Some transformations have occurred within the community, such as the University Park Campus School's commitment to training students who can give back to the neighborhood and to society at large. The arenas of transformation may differ, but one common, forward-looking vision emerges: success is measured by the skills and contributions of its graduates, not its admitted students.

These examples of democratic merit are helping us rewrite how we view achievements at commencement. More graduates are now applauded for the growth they showed in college, both in terms of their academics and their leadership abilities. They are being celebrated for their commitment to solving today's most looming challenges across an array of sectors. We can continue seeking democratic merit by measuring these students' future contributions to the public at large, rather than by simply keeping a financial scorecard. And we can apply these forward-looking criteria of democratic merit in education to cultivate more collaborative practices in society at large: from political halls, to workplaces, to service systems.

A culture shift can happen. It is happening. And we need to work together to make it happen.

ACKNOWLEDGMENTS

FIRST, I'D LIKE TO dedicate this book to my students, who have taught me more than I have taught them. I am particularly indebted to the many energetic, thoughtful, and really dedicated students with whom I worked in writing this book. These former students spent hours finding information and references; they assisted me in research, while simultaneously brainstorming ideas, working jointly with each other. They not only played key roles in developing the ideas in this book; they also demonstrated time and again the power of collaboration. Given the number of years it took to write this book, I cannot name all the students who played important roles in drafting and editing the manuscript. I can't possibly thank each of them by name, but I deeply value their contributions. However, the amazing display of diligence, energy, fortitude, and insight among the following students deserves to be noted. Indeed, without their contributions there would be no book. My special thanks go to Genzie Bonadies, Sean Braswell, Rini Fonseca, Brandon Johnson, Leah Kang, Kari Kokka, Annie Lee, Sandra Pullman, Nicole Summers, and Liliana Garces (Liliana was then a student in the Harvard Graduate School of Education; she is now an education school professor at Pennsylvania State University).

Other scholars and administrators both at Harvard Law and many other institutions have influenced and often responded to my ideas, at the same time making important contributions themselves. Many of them are cited in the text, but I especially want to thank Mahzarin

Banaji, Shirley Collado, Carol Dweck, David Labaree, Hazel Marcus, Eric Mazur, Martha Minow, Scott Page, Claude Steele, Susan Sturm, Gerald Torres, Uri Treisman, and Anita Woolley.

Because the book has been in development for almost a decade, Stuart Horwitz was also of enormous help in shaping the final manuscript, working closely with me to craft the stories I wanted to tell. I'm indebted to him. The entire team at Beacon Press has been patient and supportive, and I very much value their own commitments to collaboration.

NOTES

INTRODUCTION

1. Amartya Sen, "Merit and Justice," in *Meritocracy and Economic Inequality*, ed. Kenneth Arrow, Samuel Bowles, and Steven Durlauf (Princeton, NJ: Princeton University Press, 1999), 5, 14.

2. Michael Young, "Down with Meritocracy: The Man Who Coined the Word Four Decades Ago Wishes Tony Blair Would Stop Using It," *Guardian* (UK), June 28, 2001, http://www.theguardian.com/politics/2001/jun/29/comment.

3. Ibid.

4. The Latin word *deservire* means "to devote oneself to the service of," which in Vulgar Latin came to mean "to merit by service." Dictionary.com, http://dictionary.reference.com/search?q=desert.

CHAPTER ONE: *Adonises with a Pimple*

1. Diane Ravitch, *The Death and Life of the Great American School System: How Testing and Choice Are Undermining Education* (New York: Basic Books, 2010).

2. Fisher v. University of Texas at Austin et al., No. 11–345, 570 US, slip opinion at 1–2 (2013), http://www.supremecourt.gov/opinions/12pdf/11-345_l5gm.pdf.

3. Ibid., 1 (Thomas, J., concurring).

4. Ibid., 1–3.

5. Ibid., 18.

6. Ibid.

7. Diane Brady, *Fraternity* (New York: Random House, 2012), 50.

8. Ibid., 78.

9. Ibid., 79.

10. Ibid., 79–80.

11. Ibid.

12. Clarence Thomas, *My Grandfather's Son: A Memoir* (New York: HarperCollins, 2007), 53.

13. Ibid., 50–54.

14. Malcolm Gladwell, "Getting In," *New Yorker*, October 10, 2005, http://www.newyorker.com/archive/2005/10/10/051010crat_atlarge?currentPage=all.

15. Ibid.

16. Ibid. (Emphasis added.)

17. Ibid.

18. Robert Paul Wolff and Tobias Barrington Wolff, "The Pimple on Adonis's Nose: A Dialogue on the Concept of Merit in the Affirmative Action Debate," *Hastings Law Journal* 56 (2005). Quotes from this article were taken from pages 379, 392, 393–94, 396–97, 399, 400, and 401–2.

19. Andrew Ferguson, *Crazy U: One Dad's Crash Course in Getting His Kid into College* (New York: Simon and Schuster, 2011), 2.

20. Ibid., 185–86.

21. Beth Teitell, "College Hunt Can Bring High-Stress Summers," *Boston Globe*, March 5, 2014, https://www.bostonglobe.com/news/local/massachusetts/2014/03/05/for-high-schoolers-with-ivy-league-dreams-summer-has-gone-from-time-kick-back-time-lean/dG283mkMbZMxiIGCGu1g0M/story.html.

22. Ibid.

CHAPTER TWO: *Aptitude or Achievement?*

1. "SAT Math Practice Questions," College Board, http://sat.collegeboard.org/practice/ (last visited September 27, 2012).

2. Kaplan Test Prep, *Kaplan's Guide to the New SAT*, http://www.kaptest.com/newsat (last visited September 27, 2012).

3. Jerome Karabel, *The Chosen: The Hidden History of Admission and Exclusion at Harvard, Yale, and Princeton* (Boston: Houghton Mifflin Harcourt, 2005), 27.

4. This aristocratic Protestant value was apparent in Groton's Latin motto, "cui servire est regnare," which translates to "to serve is to reign." See Nicholas Lemann, *The Big Test: The Secret History of the American Meritocracy* (New York: Farrar, Straus and Giroux, 1999), 15.

5. See Karabel, *The Chosen*, for quotes on Ivy League admissions.

6. "The 1901 College Board (the first)," *Frontline*, http://www.pbs.org/wgbh/pages/frontline/shows/sats/where/1901.html (last visited September 27, 2012).

7. Ibid.

8. Lemann, *The Big Test*.

9. Ibid., 23–24.

10. Ibid., 30.

11. Ibid., quoting Carl C. Brigham, *A Study of American Intelligence* (1923) (internal quotation marks omitted).

12. F. Scott Fitzgerald, *The Great Gatsby* (New York: Scribner's, 1925; repr., 2004), 12–13.

13. Jon Blackwell, "1947: America's Tester-in-Chief," from *The Capital Century: 1900–1999*, http://www.capitalcentury.com/1947.html (last visited September 27, 2012).

14. Lemann, *The Big Test*, supra note 6, at 32.

15. Karabel, *The Chosen*, 141.

16. Ibid., 140.

17. Ibid.

18. Andrew Ferguson, *Crazy U: One Dad's Crash Course in Getting His Kid into College* (New York: Simon and Schuster, 2011), 86.

19. Blackwell, "1947: America's Tester-in-Chief," supra note 10.

20. Lemann, *The Big Test*, supra note 6, at 85.

21. Ibid., 273.

22. Quoted in Todd Balf, "The Story Behind the SAT Overhaul," *New York Times*, March 6, 2014, http://www.nytimes.com/2014/03/09/magazine/the-story-behind-the-sat-overhaul.html?_r=0.

23. Michele Tolela Myers, "The Cost of Bucking College Rankings," *Washington Post*, March 11, 2007, http://www.washingtonpost.com/wp-dyn/content/article/2007/03/09/AR2007030901836.html?referrer=email.

24. Ferguson, *Crazy U*, supra note 25, at 37 (internal quotation marks omitted).

25. Ibid., 43.

26. Ibid.

27. Jesse Rothstein, "College Performance Predictions and the SAT," *Journal of Econometrics* 121 (2004).

28. William C. Hiss and Valerie W. Franks, *Defining Promise: Optional Standardized Testing Policies in American College and University Admissions* (Arlington, VA: National Association for College Admission Counseling, February 5, 2014), http://www.nacacnet.org/research/research-data/nacac-research/Documents/DefiningPromise.pdf.

29. Ibid., 3.

30. Ibid., 11.

31. College Board, *2013 College-Bound Seniors: Total Group Profile Report* (New York: College Board, 2013), http://media.collegeboard.com/digitalServices/pdf/research/2013/TotalGroup-2013.pdf.

32. Ibid., 4.

33. See, for example, Maria Veronica Santelices and Mark Wilson, "Unfair Treatment? The Case of Freedle, the SAT, and the Standardization Approach to Differential Item Functioning," *Harvard Education Review* 80 (2010): 106.

34. College Board, *2013 College-Bound Seniors*, 3.

35. David K. Shipler, "My Equal Opportunity, Your Free Lunch," *New York Times*, March 5, 1995, http://www.nytimes.com/1995/03/05/weekinreview/the-nation-a-leg-up-my-equal-opportunity-your-free-lunch.html.

36. Ibid.

37. Daniel J. Hemel, "'07 Men Make More," *Harvard Crimson*, June 6, 2007, http://www.thecrimson.com/article/2007/6/6/07-men-make-more-male-harvard/.

38. Ibid.

39. Jake Freyer et al., "Class of 2013 Senior Survey," *Harvard Crimson*, May 28, 2013, http://www.thecrimson.com/flash-graphic/2013/5/28/senior-survey-2013-graphic/.

40. Ibid.

41. Leon Botstein, "SAT Is Part Hoax, Part Fraud," *Time*, March 7, 2014, 17, http://time.com/15199/college-president-sat-is-part-hoax-and-part-fraud/.

CHAPTER THREE: *From Testocratic Merit to Democratic Merit*

1. Leon Botstein, "SAT Is Part Hoax, Part Fraud," *Time*, March 7, 2014.

2. David Labaree, "Public Goods, Private Goods: The American Struggle over Educational Goals," *American Educational Research Journal* 34, no. 1 (Spring 1997): 39–81, http://www.stanford.edu/~dlabaree/publications/Public_Goods_Private_Goods.pdf.

3. Remarks delivered by Sonia Sotomayor, Associate Justice of the US Supreme Court, Princeton Alumni Day, Richardson Auditorium, February 22, 2014; Schuette v. Coalition to Defend Affirmative Action, http://www.oyez.org/cases/2010–2019/2013/2013_12_682.

4. A report on "education redlining" in Sotomayor's home town of New York City sorted all high schools in the city by state-test passage rate and found that though close to half of white and Asian students were enrolled in the top quartile of high schools, less than one-fifth of black and Hispanic students were enrolled in those top-performing schools. In the lowest quartile, in which the average student has less than a one-in-three chance of graduating in four years, black and Hispanic students were nearly four more times as likely to be enrolled as white and Asian students. None of the students in the Harlem, Bronx, and Brooklyn Community School Districts had the opportunity to learn in a high-performing school. *A Rotting Apple: Education Redlining in New York City* (Cambridge, MA: Schott Foundation

for Public Education, April 2012), http://schottfoundation.org/drupal/docs /redlining-full-report.pdf.

5. Sonia Sotomayor, *My Beloved World* (New York: Vintage, 2014), 183.

6. See Diane Brady, *Fraternity* (New York: Random House, 2012), for quotes on Holy Cross recruiting and mentoring.

7. Lyndon B. Johnson, "To Fulfill These Rights," commencement address at Howard University, June 4, 1965, http://www.lbjlib.utexas.edu/johnson/archives .hom/speeches.hom/650604.asp.

8. University of California at Irvine Office of Equal Opportunity and Diversity, "A Brief History of Affirmative Action," last updated May 3, 2010, http://www .oeod.uci.edu/aa.html.

9. Ibid., 488.

10. Ibid.

11. Jerome Karabel, *The Chosen: The Hidden History of Admission and Exclusion at Harvard, Yale, and Princeton* (Boston: Houghton Mifflin Harcourt, 2005), supra note 2 at 490.

12. Ibid.

13. Ibid., 492.

14. Ibid., 494–95.

15. "Regents of the University of California v. Bakke," Oyez Project at IIT Chicago-Kent College of Law, accessed July 13, 2014, http://www.oyez.org /cases/1970-1979/1977/1977_76_811/.

16. Ibid., 306.

17. Ibid., 279.

18. Ibid.

19. Ibid., 317.

20. Ibid.

21. Grutter v. Bollinger et al., *FindLaw*, http://caselaw.lp.findlaw.com/scripts /getcase.pl?court=US&vol=000&invol=02-241.

22. See, for example, Adam Liptak, "For Blacks in Law School, Can Less Be More?," *New York Times*, February 13, 2005, http://www.nytimes.com/2005 /02/13/weekinreview/13liptak.html; Jeff Jacoby, "The Affirmative Action Myth: Lowering Admission Standards Hurts Those It Is Supposed to Help," *Boston Globe*, December 23, 2011, http://bostonglobe.com/opinion/2011/12/23 /the-affirmative-action-myth/6WkneJSpLaoqhL3fzosPxO/story.html.

23. Brief for Abigail Fisher as Amicus Curiae Supporting Petitioner, Fisher v. University of Texas at Austin, 631 F.3d 213 (5th Cir. 2011), cert. granted (No. 11–345), http://www.law.cornell.edu/supct/cert/11-345.

24. Ibid.

25. Adam Liptak, "Race and College Admissions, Facing a New Test by Justices," *New York Times*, October 8, 2012, http://www.nytimes.com/2012/10/09/us /supreme-court-to-hear-case-on-affirmative-action.html?pagewanted=all&_r=0.

26. Ibid.

27. Critics also conveniently ignore the ways in which admissions criteria are often adjusted or disregarded for legacy students. Elite institutions have historically given children of alumni, particularly wealthy alumni, preference in the admission process. Yet those student beneficiaries are not typically scrutinized for "disidentification with academic excellence" or "low effect syndrome" to the same degree as are students of color. See, generally, Daniel Golden on this topic, including two *Wall Street Journal* articles: "Family Ties: Preference for Alumni Children in College Admission Draws Fire" (January 15, 2003), http://online.wsj.com/public/resources/documents/golden3.htm; and "College Ties: For Groton Grads, Academies Aren't Only Keys to Ivies" (April 25, 2003), http://online.wsj.com/public/resources/documents/golden1.htm; Century Foundation, "Affirmative Action for the Rich: A New Book from the Century Foundation Examines College Admissions Policies that Provide Preferences for Children of Alumni," news release, September 27, 2010, http://72.32.39.237:8080/Plone/media-center/2010/affirmative-action-for-the -rich-a-new-book-from-the-century-foundation-examines-college-admissions -policies-that-provide-preferences-for-children-of-alumni.

28. "Mission," University of Texas System, http://www.utsystem.edu/about/mission.

29. K. W. Phillips and D. L. Loyd, "When Surface and Deep-Level Diversity Collide: The Effects on Dissenting Group Members," *Organizational Behavior and Human Decision Processes* 99, no. 2 (2006): 143–60.

30. Negin R. Toosi, Samuel R. Sommers, and Nalini Ambady, "Getting a Word in Group-Wise: Effects of Racial Diversity on Gender Dynamics," *Journal of Experimental Social Psychology* 48 (2012): 115–55.

31. Denise L. Loyd et al., "Social Category Diversity Promotes Pre-meeting Elaboration: The Role of Relationship Focus," *Organization Science* 24, no. 3 (2013): 757–72.

32. Anthony Lising Antonio et al., "Effects of Racial Diversity on Complex Thinking in College Students," *Psychological Science* 15, no. 8 (2004): 507–10.

33. Samuel R. Sommers, "On Racial Diversity and Group Decision Making: Identifying Multiple Effects of Racial Composition on Jury Deliberations," *Journal of Personality and Social Psychology* 90 (2006): 597, 606.

34. S. R. Sommers, L. S. Warp, and C. C. Mahoney, "Cognitive Effects of Racial Diversity: White Individuals' Information Processing in Heterogeneous Groups," *Journal of Experimental Social Psychology* 44, no. 4 (2008): 1129–36;

Samuel R. Sommers, "Beyond Information Exchange: New Perspectives on the Benefits of Racial Diversity for Group Performance," *Research on Managing Groups and Teams* 11 (2008): 195, 206.

35. Sarah E. Gaither and Samuel R. Sommers, "Living with Other-Race Roommate Shapes Whites' Behavior in Subsequent Diverse Settings," *Journal of Experimental Social Psychology* 49, no. 2 (March 2013): 272–76.

36. It is my understanding that miners used to take a canary with them into the mine to alert them when the atmosphere in the mine was becoming poisonous. Women and blacks need to be understood as our miners' canaries: their experiences signal us about the health of our social environment. In particular, the experiences of members of these groups make visible to us fundamental flaws in the way we are distributing opportunity to everyone, but we can't see the flaws except as they are revealed by the canary. Lani Guinier, "Reframing the Affirmative Action Debate," *Kentucky Law Journal* 86, no. 505 (Spring 1997/1998), http://www.law.harvard.edu/faculty/guinier/publications/reframing_speech.pdf.

37. "Diversity Stymied," *Washington Post*, editorial, November 29, 2004, http://www.washingtonpost.com/wp-dyn/articles/A18820-2004Nov28.html.

38. In a 2004 interview, Professor Henry Louis Gates Jr. stated his belief that "[t]he black kids who come to Harvard or Yale are middle class. Nobody else gets through." Speaking on a separate occasion, Professor Gates said that 75 percent of black students at Harvard were of African or Caribbean descent or of mixed race. Gates, "Most Black Students at Harvard Are from High-Income Families," *Journal of Blacks in Higher Education* (2006), http://www.jbhe.com/news_views/52_harvard-blackstudents.html. See also Sara Rimer and Karen W. Arenson, "Top Colleges Take More Blacks but Which Ones?," *New York Times*, June 24, 2004, http://www.nytimes.com/2004/06/24/us/top-colleges-take-more-blacks-but-which-ones.html?pagewanted=all&src=pm; Douglas S. Massey et al., "Black Immigrants and Black Natives Attending Selective Colleges and Universities in the United States," *American Journal of Education* 113 (February 2007), http://www.umich.edu/~abpafs/blackimmgrants.pdf.

39. Rimer and Arenson, "Top Colleges Take More Blacks."

40. Aisha Haynie, "Not 'Just Black' Policy Considerations: The Influence of Ethnicity on Pathways to Academic Success Amongst Black Undergraduates at Harvard University," *Journal of Public and International Affairs* 13 (2002): 40–62.

41. Ibid., 43–53.

42. Ibid.

43. University Park Campus School Institute for Success, http://universitypark.worcesterschools.org/.

CHAPTER FIVE: *No Longer Lonely at the Top*

1. Rebecca Winters, "Here Comes the Lego Test," *Time*, March 4, 2001, http://content.time.com/time/nation/article/0,8599,101326,00.html.

2. Deborah Bial, "Alternative Measures for College Admissions: A Relational Study of a New Predictor for Success; the Promise of the Bial Dale College Adaptability Index and the Success of the Posse Program," PhD diss., Harvard University, 2004, p. 167.

CHAPTER SIX: *Democratic Merit in the Classroom*

1. Tina Rosenberg, *Join the Club: How Peer Pressure Can Transform the World* (New York: W. W. Norton, 2011), 100.

2. Uri Treisman, "Studying Students Studying Calculus: A Look at the Lives of Minority Mathematics Students in College," *College Mathematics Journal* 23, no. 5 (November 1992): 364–65.

3. Ibid., 366.

4. Ibid.

5. Ibid.

6. Rosenberg, *Join the Club*, 105.

7. Ibid.

8. Ibid.

9. Ibid., 367.

10. Ibid., 365.

11. Ibid., 366.

12. Ibid.

13. Ibid.

14. Philip Uri Treisman, "A Model Academic Support System," in R. Landis, ed., *Improving the Retention and Graduation of Minorities in Engineering* (New York: NACME, 1985), 56.

15. Treisman, "Studying Students Studying Calculus," 368.

16. Ibid.

17. Rosenberg, *Join the Club*.

18. Treisman, "A Model Academic Support System," 56.

19. Ibid.

20. Ibid., 57.

21. Treisman, "Studying Students Studying Calculus," 368.

22. Rosenberg, *Join the Club*, 123.

23. Treisman, "A Model Academic Support System," 56.

24. Ibid., 57.

25. Treisman, "Studying Students Studying Calculus," 369.

CHAPTER SEVEN: *Six Ways of Looking at Democratic Merit*

1. Carol S. Dweck, "The Secret to Raising Smart Kids," *Scientific American Mind* 18, no. 6 (December 2007/January 2008): 38.
2. Ibid., 38.
3. Question posed in ibid., 38.
4. Ibid., 39.
5. Janet Rae Dupree, "If You're Open to Growth, You Tend to Grow," *New York Times*, July 6, 2008, http://www.nytimes.com/2008/07/06/business/06unbox .html.
6. Dweck, "The Secret to Raising Smart Kids," 39.
7. Ibid.
8. "What Is Mindset," from the official website for Carol Dweck's book *Mindset*, retrieved November 8, 2012, http://mindsetonline.com/whatisit/about /index.html.
9. Dweck, "The Secret to Raising Smart Kids," 39.
10. Other studies conducted by Dweck and her colleagues reaffirm the finding that having a growth mind-set increases student performance. Consider the 2003 study that followed 128 premed students who were enrolled in a challenging general chemistry course.
11. Dweck, "The Secret to Raising Smart Kids," 39.
12. Paul Tough, *How Children Succeed: Grit, Curiosity, and the Power of Hidden Character* (New York: Houghton Mifflin Harcourt, 2012), xv.
13. Ibid., xiii.
14. Ibid., xv.
15. Ibid., xx.
16. Ibid., xxi.
17. Ibid., 50.
18. Ibid., 102.
19. Ibid., 56.
20. Ibid.
21. Ibid., 184.
22. Ibid.
23. Ibid., 185.
24. Graham D. Fenwick and Derrick J. Neal, "Effect of Gender Composition on Group Performance," *Gender, Work and Organization* 8, no. 2 (April 2001): 205–25, https://www.iser.essex.ac.uk/publication/504528.
25. Scott Page, prologue, *The Difference: How the Power of Diversity Creates Better Groups, Firms, Schools, and Societies* (Princeton, NJ: Princeton University Press, 2007).

26. Lu Hong and Scott E. Page, "Groups of Diverse Problem Solvers Can Outperform Groups of High-Ability Problem Solvers," William J. Baumol, ed., *Proceedings of the National Academy of Sciences* 101, no. 46 (November 16, 2004): 16385–89.

27. Marilynn B. Brewer and Wendi Gardner, "Who Is This 'We'? Levels of Collective Identity and Self-representations," *Journal of Personality and Social Psychology* 71, no. 1 (1996): 86.

28. All school, student, and teacher names in this chapter are pseudonyms.

29. Jo Boaler and Megan Staples, "Creating Mathematical Futures Through an Equitable Teaching Approach: The Case of Railside School," *Teachers College Record* 110, no. 3 (2008): 608–45.

30. Ibid., 613.

31. Railside's "reform oriented" approach used small-group work; students presented to the class and worked on longer, more conceptual tasks than students in the "traditional" math classes, where lecture and individual practice consumed the majority of class time.

32. Boaler and Staples, "Creating Mathematical Futures," 620.

33. Railside students outperformed Greendale and Hilltop students on assessments administered by the research study, on district assessments, and on the California Standards Test of algebra but did not outperform them on the CAT 6, a state standardized test, nor on indicators of Adequate Yearly Progress. Boaler offers hypotheses for this discrepancy, such as the cultural and linguistic barriers characteristic of the standardized state and federal assessments (ibid., 624).

34. California does not require high school students to take mathematics for all four years.

35. Boaler and Staples, "Creating Mathematical Futures," 621.

36. Ibid., 622.

37. Ibid., 621.

38. Ibid., 637.

39. Ibid.

40. Jo Boaler, "Promoting 'Relational Equity' and High Mathematics Achievement Through an Innovative Mixed Ability Approach," *British Educational Research Journal* 34, no. 2 (2008): 167–94.

41. Elizabeth G. Cohen and Rachel A. Lotan, "Producing Equal-Status Interaction in the Heterogeneous Classroom," *American Educational Research Journal* 32, no. 1 (1995): 99–120.

42. Boaler and Staples, "Creating Mathematical Futures," 619.

43. Ibid., 630.

44. Elizabeth G. Cohen and Rachel A. Lotan, *Working for Equity in Heterogeneous Classrooms: Sociological Theory in Practice*, Sociology of Education Series (New York: Teachers College Press, 1997).

45. Boaler and Staples, "Creating Mathematical Futures," 634.

46. Ibid., 631.

47. Boaler, "Promoting 'Relational Equity,'" 184.

48. Ibid., 167–68.

49. Ibid., 185.

50. The only achievement difference that did persist at Railside was the higher performance of Asian American students versus their black and Latino peers.

CHAPTER EIGHT: *Democratic Merit in a Twenty-First-Century World*

1. Charles McGrath, "Atul Gawande Rocks the E.R.," *New York Times*, April 3, 2007, http://www.nytimes.com/2007/04/03/books/03atul.html?pagewanted=all&_r=0.

2. Atul Gawande, "The Cost Conundrum," *New Yorker*, June 1, 2009, http://www.newyorker.com/reporting/2009/06/01/090601fa_fact_gawande?currentPage=all.

3. World Health Organization, *The World Health Report 2000: Health Systems; Improving Performance* (Geneva: World Health Organization, 2000), http://www.who.int/whr/2000/en/whr00_en.pdf.

4. Stephen C. Schoenbaum et al., *Mirror, Mirror on the Wall: An International Update on the Comparative Performance of American Health Care* (New York: Commonwealth Fund, May 1, 2007), http://www.commonwealthfund.org/usr_doc/1027_davis_mirror_mirror_international_update_final.pdf.

5. Gawande, "The Cost Conundrum."

6. Ibid.

7. Ibid.

8. Ibid.

9. Ibid.

10. Ibid.

11. For quotes on his research, see Archon Fung, "Street Level Democracy: A Theory of Popular Pragmatic Deliberation and Its Practice in Chicago School Reform and Community Policing, 1988–1997," PhD diss., Massachusetts Institute of Technology, 2000.

INDEX